An Expression of Pedagogy

A Theory of Acceptable Losses: Elements of the African-American Diaspora

BY SHERMAN BONDS, ED.D.

The contents of this work, including, but not limited to, the accuracy of events, people, and places depicted; opinions expressed; permission to use previously published materials included; and any advice given or actions advocated are solely the responsibility of the author, who assumes all liability for said work and indemnifies the publisher against any claims stemming from publication of the work.

All Rights Reserved
Copyright © 2021 by Sherman Bonds, Ed.D.

No part of this book may be reproduced or transmitted, downloaded, distributed, reverse engineered, or stored in or introduced into any information storage and retrieval system, in any form or by any means, including photocopying and recording, whether electronic or mechanical, now known or hereinafter invented without permission in writing from the publisher.

Dorrance Publishing Co
585 Alpha Drive
Pittsburgh, PA 15238
Visit our website at *www.dorrancebookstore.com*

ISBN: 978-1-6495-7167-0
eISBN: 978-1-6495-7676-7

Acknowledgments

I considered myself a Missourian. I came to Missouri in 1960. I left Missouri in 1981. For twenty-one years, I lived in this state. I grew up in Sikeston, Missouri, the Boot-hill as some may know. I traveled throughout the Boot-hill as a child, often visiting towns such as Charleston, Hayti, Lilbourn, Essex, Dexter, Caruthersville, Popular Bluff, East Prairie, Kenneth, Steele, Benton, Cape Girardeau, and many other small-town communities. In other words, I am speaking and writing from a rural perspective about my experiences and how this relates to my matriculation at Lincoln University of Missouri.

I was reared and educated in this state. Throughout my upbringing, I saw, up close, what impoverished conditions looked like and what my personal experiences taught me as a person of color. I grew up learning how to go to the fields to chop beans, bail hay, pick watermelon, pick strawberries, and pick corn. I was there when they put the first bathtub in our house when they brought the first gas line to our neighborhood. Our house stood on cinder blocks. I grew up with a wood/coal burning stove. We lived off the fat of the land. Our meat, well, we fished and hunted wild game, and yes, we ate venison. We would get our school clothes once a year, including shoes. Sometimes we went barefoot, and yes, I have stumped my toe, meaning I knocked off my big toenail, a very painful experience. I traveled and walked dirt and rocky roads throughout the Boot-hill region.

School, well, I started out at our neighborhood school. Our school's name was Lincoln, and it served students in grades one through twelve. We only had that one school for blacks, and it was a segregated school. Although Brown v. Board of Education had passed in 1954, integration for Sikeston came when I entered the third grade in 1963. I was sent to Southwest Elementary School in the white neighborhood, and they closed our school. No whites came to our neighborhood to go to school. Integration was one-sided. We went to their neighborhood schools, but they (whites) did not come to our community.

I grew up regurgitating what they taught me in school. I learned what they valued in their broader culture. In rural Missouri, we learned to square dance, listen to their music, and we sang their songs. The entire cultural experience was positioned within a dominant white cultural model. Our high school prom king and queen were white, and they positioned their cultural experiences above ours on every front. Education within our schools was not a prevalent factor beyond the secondary level. We were encouraged to take up a trade. Post-secondary development was not presented to me on a massive scale. It came about as a young lady across the street from where I lived thought enough to suggest to me that I, too, could go to college, and that college was Lincoln University. I desired and sought for an experience that would give me a place to grow and learn and one that would be culturally sensitive to my development. Yes, one could say I was in search of myself, and I needed a Lincoln to do just that. Harvard and Oxford University were not within my lexicon, yet I am favored for these thoughts after great reflection about Lincoln University.

- ✓ My hopes and dreams are garnered through the prism of the sacrifices made by the men of the 62nd and 65th Colored Infantry who sought out a place for me to pursue this indelible aspiration of hope.
- ✓ It is here, upon this hill, that I forged a new beginning that is like no other, for here is where I set my mark upon the world, and I know that my scholarly realm will always follow me where ever I go.
- ✓ Now that I have arrived, knowing fully that I must depart, let it be known that I walked through the halls of a redeeming place where I stimulated my inner peace and now my soul speaks of tranquility. It was here, at Lincoln, that I acquired these majestic ideals for achievement.
- ✓ To acquire formal education, you first must find a place that exemplifies that for which you seek. Here at Lincoln, I found an example of leadership that epitomizes no other. Our history is grounded in the belief that "I can learn that which I do not know and earn a degree that I do not have."
- ✓ They came after me, and I said yes, I will come and I will excel. They said this is their watch and you are under our care. Therefore to all who read this passage, thank you because the village that surrounds me is forever nurturing my development as a scholar.

Furthermore let it be known that I understand the dilemma of poor European (whites) Americans. They, too, were marginalized by the great society, and Lincoln University embraced them, too. Therefore let us not remove our legacy as a moment gone by in history, but help them (whites) understand that they, too, can embrace our quest to bring forward a diverse institution of higher education without sacrificing our African-American history and placing it in the annals of the past. Lincoln is a historically black college/university, and it should be celebrated by all who enter its realm. Lincoln is now a part of the pedagogy that we practice, no longer a one-sided pronouncement. We have a story to tell our children, yet it should be told to everyone.

You see, Lincoln was and is more than just a post-secondary platform where students come to grow and learn. It is now a part of the African-American Diaspora (culture) and its preservation is paramount. Lincoln restores the Negro, Colored, black man, and African-American heritage and reconnects its historical lineage to a culture that was once separated by slavery. I close this treatise by offering some of my writings for you to read. I hope that they will add to your understanding of the importance of Lincoln and the footprint that it brings to Missouri and our nation. The following writings are my expressions of thought, and they reflect what I teach to the children that I serve and support. As an alumnus, I have assisted over 125 students in gaining entrance to Lincoln University and several have graduated.

An Expression of Pedagogy

A Theory of Acceptable Losses:
Elements of the African-American Diaspora

Table of Contents

Foreword xi
Prologue xix
A Theory of Acceptable Losses: Elements of the African American Diasporas ... xxi
Introduction 1
The African American Women – A Great Reflection of Gospel 43
When I Was Shamed 47
If the Trees Could Talk 49
From the Shoulders, I Stand On 51
Remembering and Honoring Our Elders 53
I am a Black Woman in Training 55
Who am I 57
The Negro's Epilogue 59
The Inauguration and Black History 63
I am Black History – A Childs Story 67
I Wonder 69
Just a Boy an Innocent Child 71
I was Born a Negro 73
What am I Made of 75
Why Should I Care About the Past 77
Wearing it Tight 79
Working Without a Kingmaker 83
I Come with Scars 85
What Do You Do When – The Pedagogy is Hijacked by Syllogism 87
Bibliography 97
Book Reviews 103

Foreword

A Personal Story Concerning American History

On May 17th, 1954, the United States Supreme Court handed down the Brown v. Board of Topeka 347 U.S. 483 (1954) decision. This landmark decision overturned the previous ruling set down by the U.S. Supreme Court under Plessy v. Ferguson of 1896, where it applied to public education. Our nation then lived under the legal policy of separate but equal. Nineteen months later, I would take my first breath of life. However, this important day came twenty-five days just after Mrs. Rosa Louise McCauley Parks refused to give up her seat on a bus in Montgomery, Alabama December 1955. Eleven months after my birth, in November 1956, the United States Supreme Court upheld the ruling set down by the Federal District Court in Browder v. Gayle, where they ruled that bus segregation was unconstitutional. During this timeline, a new beginning had been established by the U.S. Supreme Court. A new era had commenced, and life as a youth for me and many others, both black and white, set the stage for a new interpretation for civil liberties. Separate but equal in the public classroom had been struck down, and segregation on public transportation was ruled unconstitutional.

I began my educational experience in 1962 in a segregated school. I was promoted to the third grade at the end of the school year in 1965. But before I would enter this school, I could recall then the political climate of the day. From 1953 to 1961, Dwight D. Eisenhower served as the 34th President of the United States of America and Richard M. Nixon served as his Vice President. My grandparents, who held no more than a second or third-grade education, expressed considerable value upon their children and grandchildren for obtaining a high school education. College was a sizeable leap for them to consider and/or imagine. Yet they expressed to me their hopes and dreams to see one of their offspring meet this objective.

John F. Kennedy symbolized their ideals and aspirations during this time. Voting for blacks and/or African-Americans was still hampered by the negative effects of what was described as the Jim Crow Laws. You see, Jim Crow was not a real person but an idea or caricature that bore roots in American culture.

> The term "Jim Crow" typically refers to repressive laws and customs once used to restrict black rights, but the origin of the name itself actually dates back to before the Civil War. In the early 1830s, the white actor Thomas Dartmouth "Daddy" Rice was propelled to stardom for performing minstrel routines as the fictional "Jim Crow," a caricature of a clumsy, dimwitted black slave. Rice claimed to have first created the character after witnessing an elderly black man singing a tune called "Jump Jim Crow" in Louisville, Kentucky. He later appropriated the Jim Crow persona into a minstrel act where he donned blackface and performed jokes and songs in a stereotypical slave dialect. For example, "Jump Jim Crow" included the popular refrain, "Weel about and turn about and do 'jis so, eb'ry time I weel about I jump Jim Crow." Rice's minstrel act

proved a massive hit among white audiences, and he later took it on tour around the United States and Great Britain. As the show's popularity spread, "Jim Crow" became a widely used derogatory term for blacks.

Jim Crow's popularity as a fictional character eventually died out, but in the late 19th century, the phrase found new life as a blanket term for a wave of anti-black laws laid down after Reconstruction. Some of the most common laws included restrictions on voting rights—many Southern states required literacy tests or limited suffrage to those whose grandfathers had also had the right to vote—bans on interracial relationships and clauses that allowed businesses to separate their black and white clientele. The segregationist philosophy of "separate but equal" was later upheld in the famous 1896 Supreme Court decision "Plessy vs. Ferguson," in which the Court ruled that the state of Louisiana had the right to require different railroad cars for blacks and whites. The "Plessy" decision would eventually lead to widespread adoption of segregated restaurants, public bathrooms, water fountains, and other facilities. "Separate but equal" was eventually overturned in the 1954 Supreme Court Case "Brown vs. Board of Education," but Jim Crow's legacy would continue to endure in some Southern states until the 1970s. (http://www.history.com/news/ask-history/was-jim-crow-a-real-person)

In 1960, John Fitzgerald Kennedy was elected as the 35th President of the United States of America, and Lyndon Baines Johnson served as his vice-presidential running mate. Sworn into office in January of 1961 President Kennedy's life was cut short by an assassin bullet on November 22, 1963, and Vice President Lyndon Baines Johnson was sworn into office as our 36th President of the United State of America. I can't really say if my grandparents voted for Kennedy or not, but what I do remember is the school that I would later attend was designated as the voting place where people in our community cast their ballots for elections. I entered this school (Lincoln) before integration was applied, even though the law had been set-down outlawing segregation in public schools. The year was fall 1962, seven years after the Brown v. Board of Topeka decision, I entered a segregated school. Mr. Ford was my principal. I know he was an accomplished man and held an advanced degree. I know because my grandmother would often tell me this is what she wished I would someday acquire.

Kennedy had not yet been killed by an assassin's bullet. His picture was hung in our house as a reminder of an emerging symbol of hope. Two more years would pass, and I would be promoted to the third grade, and now I would be enrolled in an integrated school (Southwest Elementary). President Kennedy's death came during my second year in school, and a great deal of sadness surrounded our home. Hope from years past had seemed to dissipate, and the hours lay upon my shoulders from where we would go from here as a people. Living in a rural community where one would labor in the fields, chopping beans, picking various vegetables, and cleaning other people's houses for daily living expenses, my grandparents wanted more for me than this.

Education was the drumbeat, sounding and resounding again and again by my grandparents. Hope for our future was predicated on my ability to reach a new milestone, and that milestone was for me to graduate from high school and go to college and earn a college degree. A tall order for the time! Jim Crow, a mythical heading, held its roots in an American culture who thought very little about the inalienable rights of life, liberty, and the pursuit of happiness for a people of color, let alone a black and/or African-American child. However, the death of a president would significantly impact a nation's consciousness, and to this end, the new civil rights era emerged.

Ten years had passed now since the Brown v. Board of Topeka decision became law, and old Jim Crow was holding on for dear life. Public sit-ins were now a commonplace, and public marches were heralded as the place to protest against a faltered interposition for racial separation among the American populace. President Johnson was faced with a significant challenge. Were we all created equal? Do we all have access to that which is endowed by our creator? Questions such as these were evidenced by the people who gathered in the streets for a public protest; by those who sat in public venues and quietly submitted themselves to public humiliation. They were those who one could say, we are who we are, a people of color, who for many years have suffered the internal damnation of a cruel society just because of the color of our skin. Enough is enough! A decade does not seem that long to some, but then I was only in the third grade, and history tells me the Civil War began April 12, 1861, and ended April 9, 1865 at Appomattox Court House in Appomattox, Virginia.

An irony or a paradox! It appears one hundred years later, the argument prevailed. The Civil Rights Act of 1964 introduced by President Kennedy, and subsequently passed under the leadership of President Johnson, provided the framework to lay old Jim Crow to rest. Although the Civil Rights Act of 1964 made it illegal to discriminate against people based on his/her race, color, religion, sex, or national origin, and where the act further gave relief for unequal application of voter registration requirements and racial segregation in schools, at the workplace, and in public places; President Johnson would still need to get Congress to pass the Voter Rights Act of 1965 before old Jim Crow would give up the ghost completely (see Public

Law 88-352-Civil Rights Act-July 2, 1964 and Public Law 89-110-Voting Rights Act-August 6, 1965). I think "Bloody Sunday" may have awakened a nation where they saw the brutal character of a mythical figure (Jim Crow) unfold before their very eyes.

Before I completed elementary school, all of this had taken place, and I was one of the many who was being developed to go forward in the existence of clear and present danger. What danger one may ask! The idea of an educated African-American populace was terrifying to some. Upon until now, they who opposed such a new development had always relied on their internal fears and beliefs that to be inclusive in a democratic society did not mean they should afford these liberties to the offspring of former slaves. Although I moved to an integrated school, my community lost much. How much? It's difficult to measure. My former school was not among the schools that were integrated. No white student came to our community to go to school. We had to go to their schools in their communities. Our school was closed. We lost our educational leader because the local school board wanted to demote him to the level of Assistant Principal. He (Mr. Ford) moved away and relocated to Kansas City, Missouri.

I guess they (local school board official and others) thought a decade was not long enough, or even a century, especially if it meant placing a black man and/or African-American as the Principal of a local school where white children would attend. This kind of thinking and the process for integration was not just limited to my community; it was applied across the nation, particularly in the mid-western and southern states of our nation. In part one may apply this scenario toward the thinking for some of the greater populace in our nations' history.

My grandmother's great-great-mother was a slave, and one day she told her master that she was hungry. Well, the master said bring me a hog. Her master took the hog and hung it from a limb somewhere near the barn, then he cut the hog's belly right in the center and pulled out its guts and dropped them at her feet and said go eat that, and she did. Later she came back and said master, I am hungry, and the master cut the four feet from the hog and said go eat that, and she did. She then returns and said master, I am still hungry, and the master cut the hog's tail off and the hog's ears and said go and eat that, and she did. Now my great-great-great-grandmother returned one last time, and said master I am hungry, and the last thing the master cut from that old hog was his snoot (nose), and he gave it to her and said now go eat that, and she did. The moral of this story is this; I am made of chitterlings, hog maws, pig feet, pigtails, pig ears, and barbecue snoot, and I am the offspring of a slave who raised her children with hope.

Now I turn your attention to the paradox for inclusion when fighting racial segregation. I want you to go to your house and get your mother's crystal pitcher and fill it with water. Then I want you to take that pitcher of water and allow a hungry dog who you just saw eating its own feces drink from it because he had no food to eat or water to drink. Go ahead, give him a drink. Now I want you to take a drink from that same pitcher of water that you just allowed that dog to drink from. Repulsed! Well, now you can imagine how some white people felt when they saw me drinking from the public water fountain in the park. Being viewed for being no less than a dog and emerging on the doorsteps of my grandparent's dreams, some felt my aspirations were too great to accomplish.

Ten-years-old I applied myself, and yes, I finished school. I went far as I could, I went all the way. I earned my high school diploma in May 1975. I then earned my Bachelor of Science degree in Psychology in 1980. Thereafter I earned my first master's degree in Sociology/Criminal Justice in 1980 and my second master's degree in Special

Education in June 1998. I completed my educational journey in May of 2002 by earning my Doctor of Education degree in Educational Leadership. Oh, yeah, I did complete a post doctorate leadership experience at both Harvard University and Manchester College at the University of Oxford in Oxford, England.

Prologue

The work of *An Expression of Pedagogy and The African-American Consciousness* offers a central perspective for the recapitulation of an African-American's thought. In this body of work, the author explores, — *A Theory of Acceptable Losses: Elements of The African-American Diasporas."* This acceptable loss to humanity would be the former Negro slave and his/her offspring. The basis of the theory is grounded in the historical postulation of America's birth as a nation. The underpinning of a great society forged through a hypocritical thesis regarding democracy is disclosed. The flaws of the founding fathers of American democracy are captured through the author's lens of how this theory began and continues today. The compounding framework for the imperialist nomenclature of European thought undergirds this treatise.

> From the age of kings to the crude elements of fascism, the consciousness of a nation is suppressed for generations. The essential characteristics of one society are laid wasted at the behest of unfortunate people. Retelling this story in this format may give rise to a new awareness of thought as we move through the new millennium. And for others, it may give them a new understanding of the African-American struggle in

American society. Liberty for some and not for all is no liberty at all. This body of work further provides African-Americans and others a more detailed description of the pedagogy that is practiced when history is made new to an enlightened reader.

Literacy, nobility, and honor, all of which are valued by men and women, should be celebrated, and the African-American story is an essential part of this quest. The author will also state this is our grandmother's story retold from the grave in which she lays. The *Reflective Thoughts Toward an African-American Heritage* are writings given to children of African descent. To encourage a mind to reach outside the realms of proximity and draw close to his or her being is another essential quality of human consciousness. It is the author's belief these writings can bring pause for critical thinking about African-American history in the world as we know it today. Enjoy your readings, and may you be challenged to think differently.

A Theory of Acceptable Losses:
Elements of the African-American Diasporas

In these bloody days and frightful nights when an urban warrior can find no face more despicable than his own, no ammunition more deadly than self-hate and no target deserving of his true aim than his brother, we must wonder how we come to so late and lonely to this place.

MAYA ANGELOU,
*As Cited In -The Warrior Method
by Raymond A. Winbush, Ph.D., 2001, p.6.*

Introduction

A Theory of Acceptable Losses: Elements of the African-American Diasporas is an attempt to review and revisit the American tragedy of democracy and freedom for people of color. The transformation of humanity to an ill form of inhumane suffering placed upon the Africans who were brought to America during the seventeenth century rests at the center of this theoretical postulate and framework. The author begins by examining the terms Negro and Black as the beginning of the transformation for the dehumanization of the African-American continuum. Embedded in the African-American Diasporas are the negative stereotypical formations brought forward through the slave trade in the western hemisphere. The term Diaspora means the scattering of language, culture, or people: a dispersion of a people, language, or culture that was formerly concentrated in one place, the African Diaspora‖ (*Encarta ® World English Dictionary* 1998-2005).

    The author raises the question about the term "Negro" and the descriptive attributes associated with the being that is described. The term Negro is a noun that was utilized as an adjective to disconnect the Africans' consciousness to his or her existence as a human being. Therefore this usage of the term Negro is more easily conferred as the chattels personal or, for this examination, <u>chattel-person-syndrome</u>

of the seventeenth century that was brought forward in America. In the text of *Slavery in America*, Kenneth M. Stampp defines *"Chattels Personal"* as moveable personal property (p.82, 2001). Chattel includes any moveable property, such as animals, livestock, and any other article that is moveable (*The World Book Encyclopedia*, p. 331, 1965). For centuries the term Negro and Black were applied to the African-American identity culminating in the total demise of any conscious memory of his/her African culture. This symbolic transformation was carried forward throughout the seventeenth, eighteenth, nineteenth, and twentieth centuries, both in America and abroad. And today it still remains as the most destructive module for a nation's consciousness when describing the African-American experience.

To illustrate this paradox, the author presents this framework for consideration. To be politically correct, a person may use the term European-American when speaking of the Whites who came from Europe (England, France, Germany, or Scotland). Asian-Americans would be those Americans whose forefathers' homelands are found in China, Japan, or Korea. And Native Americans would be those individuals whose fathers and mothers were born on this soil called America. Now the Negro, where is his land? Stripped of conscious connections, the Negro is situated in the abyss—no land, no language, no (Diasporas) culture. This descriptive analysis places the African species at the lowest and most undesirable position for human identification and/or recognition. Stampp, 2001, recited this expression:

> In other societies, such as Russia in past centuries, many agricultural workers lived in conditions very like slavery. They could not own land, relocate, or disobey orders from a landowner. Nonetheless Russian peasants were seen as individuals, as persons, they could

not be sold, given away, or forced from their homes. This was not the case in America (p. 82).

Thus, the question comes to bear: Who is the Negro, the Black man, and the African-American? The Negro was the slave, the Black man was the emancipator, and the African-American became the conscious of America. While freedom for the Negro slave was stricken from the Declaration of Independence in 1776, the Declaration remains as the centerpiece for a nation that describes itself as a symbol for freedom and democracy (see *The Writings of Thomas Jefferson: Being His Autobiography, Correspondence, Reports, Messages, Addresses, and Other Writings, Official and Private, Washington, D.C.: Taylor & Maury, 1953-1854*, as cited at http://www.blackpast.org/primary/declaration-independence-and-debate-over-slavery).

Even through this hypocrisy, under the disguise of a democratic society, America forged ahead and built a great nation on the shoulders of a chattel people whom they thought to be unworthy of citizenship and/or human identification. These men and women of African descent, given the position of chattel status, were considered to be *"acceptable losses,"* so that a nation such as America could be born. How could this happen? Historians have specific dates, however, this author has a theory. What is a theory? According to the definition found in *The American Heritage Dictionary, 2nd CollegeEdition,*1985, p. 1260: *Theory* is defined as 1. a "Systematically organized knowledge applicable in a relatively wide variety of circumstances, esp. a system of assumptions, accepted principles, and rules of procedure devised to analyze, predict, or otherwise explain the nature of the behavior of a specified set of phenomena." Adding to this, one may refer to the definition provided by Gall, Gall & Borg, 1999, p. 553: "Theory – An explanation of particular phenomena in terms of a set of underlying constructs and a set of principles that relates the constructs to each other."

In this treatise, the author begins to develop this theory of acceptable losses by correlating the phenomena of democracy for some people but not for all based on racial factors alone. Embedded in this theory are the constructs to build an independent nation that will use capitalism as its basis for economic prosperity for some but not for all, and race becomes the element of disguise. The theory of acceptable losses is presented through the descriptive facts under the term imperialism or imperialistic power. Imperialism is defined as:

> (1) belief in empire-building: the policy of extending the rule or influence of a country over other countries or colonies;
>
> (2) domination by empire: the political, military, or economic domination of one country over another; and
>
> (3) takeover and domination: the extension of power or authority over others in the interests of domination cultural imperialism (*Encarta ® World English Dictionary* 1998-2005).

The context of this imperialistic view has always been romanticized in English and European folklore. Examples can be brought forward from the days of Caesar and the domination of Roman power. Often excluded yet sometimes reviewed are the days of Pharaohs, Egyptian Kings not often spoken of in the African context, given no rise to superior power or domination of the African descent or its continent.

From the days of Pharaohs and Caesars, we move to the land of England, where the modern form of an English monarchy was born. In this land, there was a Crown where the monarchy was made up of a king and queen, prince and princess, duke and duchess, and finally the House of Lords. Beneath this line were the servants to the Crown.

Impenetrable and only through bloodlines, the servant (commoner/peasant) was forever indebted to the Crown. The land and all possessions belonged to the Crown. The servant had no aristocracy; his or her solitary order of the day was to preserve the aristocracy of the Crown. Possessed with nothing, the servant was beholden to the English monarchy. Deeply embedded in the English monarchy was the notion of imperialistic power. Those dominated by the power of the English were enslaved and made into servants of the lands the English conquered. You see, slavery was not associated with color until it reached the western shores of America (Hoffman, 1992). All people, regardless of color, were subject to the imperialistic rule of their captors.

However, in most historical cases today, we do not recall and/or recite particular aspects of this imperialistic nomenclature to be set upon and acted against whites. This subterfuge has been and remains a delicate matter of presentation. In fact history discloses such an act and condition.

White Slavery in Ancient & Medieval Europe

> Among the ancient Greeks, despite their tradition of democracy, the enslavement of fellow whites, even fellow Greeks—was the order of the day. Aristotle considered White slaves as things. The Romans also had no compunctions against enslaving Whites who they, too, termed "a thing" *(res)*. In his agricultural writings, the first century B.C. Roman philosopher Varro labeled White slaves as nothing more than "tools that happened to have voices" *(instrumental vocal)*. Cato the Elder, discoursing on plantation management, proposed that white slaves, when old or ill, should be discarded along with worn-out farm implements.
>
> Julia Caesar enslaved as many as one million whites from Gaul, some of whom were sold to the slave

dealers who followed his victorious legions (William D. Phillips, Jr., *Slavery from Roman Times to the Early Transatlantic Trade*, p. 18).

In A.D. [*sic Year of our Lord*] 319, the "Christian" emperor of Rome, Constantine, ruled that if an owner whipped his white slave to death, "he should not stand in any criminal accusation if the slave dies; and all the statutes of limitations and legal interpretations are hereby set aside."

The Romans enslaved thousands of the early white inhabitants of Great Britain who were known as "Angles," from which we derive the term "Anglo-Saxon" as a description of the English race. In the sixth century [*sic 500 A.D. – Year of our Lord*], Pope Gregory the First witnessed blond-haired, blue-eyed English boys awaiting sale in a slave market in Rome (as cited in Hoffman II, 1992, p. 7).

Even with this historical digest, English folklore continued this romanticism through the subjectivity of discovering America. With the earlier teaching of Christopher Columbus' discovery of America in 1492, the concept of imperial rule subsumed this nation called America. Given the distance from the imperial ruler (the Crown), servants and slaves were sent to a faraway land to continue the behest of an oppressor.

Whites Were the First Slaves in America

The enslavement of whites extended throughout the American colonies, and white slave labor was a crucial factor in the economic development of the colonies. Gradually it developed into a fixed system every bit as

> rigid and codified as Negro slavery was to become. In fact Negro slavery was efficiently established in colonial America because black slaves were governed, organized, and controlled by the structures and organizations that were first used to enslave and control whites. Black slaves were "latecomers fitted into a system already developed" (Ulrich B. Phillips, Life, and Labor in the Old South, pp. 25-26).
>
> White slavery was the historic base upon which Negro slavery was constructed. "…the important structure, labor, ideologies, and social relations necessary for slavery already had been established within indentured servitude…white servitude…in many ways came remarkably close to the 'ideal type' of chattel slavery, which later became associated with the African experience" (Hilary McD. Beckles, *White Servitude*, pp. 6-7 and 71). "The practice developed and tolerated in the kidnapping of whites laid the foundation for the kidnapping of Negroes" (Eric Williams, From Columbus to Castro, p. 103). As cited in Hoffman II, 1992, p. 47).

As cited above, during this time, the servant or slave was referred to as the indentured servant indebted to his master and/or captive. Hoffman continues this description as cited below.

> The American colonies prospered through the use of white slaves, which Virginia planter John Pory declared in 1619 "our principal wealth."
>
> "The white servant, a semi-slave, was more important in the 17th century than even the Negro slave, with respect to both numbers and economic significance" (Marcus W. Jernegan, *Laboring and Dependent Classes in Colonial America*, p. 45).

> Where mainstream history books or films touch on white slavery, it is referred to with the deceptively mild-sounding title of "indentured servitude," the implication being that the enslavement of whites was not as terrible or all-encompassing as negro "slavery" but constituted instead more benign bondage, that of "servitude."
>
> Yet the terms servant and slave were often used interchangeably to refer to people whose status was clearly that of permanent, lifetime enslavement. "An Account of the English Sugar Plantacons" (sic) in the British Museum (Stowe manuscript) written circa 1660-1685, refers to black and white slaves as "servants:" "…the Colonyes were plentifully supplied with Negro and Christian servants, which are nerves and sinews of a plantacon…" (Christian was a euphemism for white). (As cited in Hoffman II, 1992, p. 47-48).

In either case, America belonged to the Crown of England, and for years to come, the English would unload its citizenry in the New World. According to history, those to be punished for crimes against the Crown were banished to the New World. The English and other European forces continued their quest to populate the land of the native son. The native son was given his name by the English—Indian. The Indian once sought out as an ally for this new nation would later be conquered by the rule of imperial power. This level of invasion continued for centuries, which brings us to the seventeenth century and the years of 1600. During this period in history, slavery had become a lucrative market and a form of cheap labor in the West Indies. New terms are introduced in America and abroad: the Middle Passage‖ (slave route), chattel personal‖ (moveable property), and white supremacy (domination over another by race). The color of a man's skin had become the common distinction between that of a superior being versus that of one who would be inferior by race alone. Notwithstanding the servants' position, the Crown still remained the superior class elitist both in America and abroad.

This analysis exhibits the specific distinction between the servant and that of the slave— race. Both were subjects of the Crown, neither had an aristocracy of their own. American history places the birth of this relationship in the State of Virginia and the town called Jamestown. Both the servant and the slave were penniless. However, the context of the servant places the slave in an indignant position, chattel personal, where he is stripped of his dignity, robbed of his language, and torn loose from his heritage. Lowered to a status beneath that of a dog, the Negro was formed. Beaten, torched, maimed, and killed, the Negro and elements of the African Diasporas were changed forever.

Although the servant favors the position of a superior being, he still must resolve his status; he had nor possessed anything of inherent value. The servant, no better than a slave, uneducated, illiterate, was reminded continuously that he remained the subject of the Crown and could be treated without dignity or retribution as a slave. This particular aspect of American history can best be analyzed through the lens of Georgia's Charter, as the 13th Colony in America. The romantic interlude was driven by the destitute of the poor English peasant. James Edward Oglethorpe, an English nobleman, was a member of Parliament's House of Commons.

> During that time, England was faced with many problems. There were more people than there were jobs. Many citizens, some well-known ones, could not pay their debts. Laws concerning debtors were strict and harsh, and those who could not pay went to jail. Among those jailed was Oglethorpe's friend, architect Robert Castell.

Oglethorpe was shocked at the inhumane treatment of debtors he visited in prison and wanted to pass laws to help them. Not only were thousands arrested each year for not paying their debts, but many were charged a fee for being in jail. The death of his friend, Robert Castell, while in debtor's prison led Oglethorpe to demand reforms.

In the summer of 1730, Oglethorpe's group of twenty-one men asked King George II for a tract of land on the "southwest of Carolina for settling poor persons of London." Georgia, like other American colonies, would offer religious freedom to Protestants, who were being mistreated by the Catholic Church in Europe. Too, the King liked the idea of more land and greater power for England.

On June 7, 1732, King George II granted a charter making Oglethorpe's group of twenty-one trustees responsible for establishing the colony of Georgia and for managing it for twenty-one years.

The charter had six thousand words and many limits. The King stated that the trustees could not own land, hold political office, or be given money for their work. "Papist" (Catholics), blacks, liquor dealers, and lawyers could not become colonists.

The colony belonged to the Crown, so the trustees were to get instructions from King George II. They could pass no laws unless the King agreed. King George limited the trustees' authority, made them managers for a definite period of time, and said they could make no profit. As cited in *Georgia – The History of an American State*, 1999, pp. 96-100.

Prior to the writing of the Declaration of Independence, colonists revealed this very notion about the servant through their pronouncement to the English Parliament against taxation without representation. No better than a slave uneducated, illiterate, and where intellectual prowess was left to the nobles emerged the beginning of the American aristocracy: Harvard University was founded in 1636 and then came William and Mary in 1693. Some could argue these institutions of higher education brought with them the foundation for the birth of an American aristocracy. Often we read that the founding fathers were educated men. And we know John Adams, one of the fifty-six signers of the Declaration of Independence, graduated from Harvard University in 1755 and the principal architect of our historic declaration, Thomas Jefferson, earned his college degree from The College of William and Mary in 1762.

As the servant moved forward with his educational achievements, the idea of developing a free nation materialized. Former loyalists of European (white) descent and servants to the Crown gathered to discuss their independence from the Crown. Shackled by tyranny, the former European loyalist and servant wrote a decree entitled the Declaration of Independence in the State of Pennsylvania and the city of Philadelphia. These men from the thirteen colonies gathered in 1776 and brought forward this historical decree but without freeing the Negro slave.

According to history, the gentlemen from South Carolina [*Edward Rutledge, Arthur Middleton, Thomas Lynch, Jr., Thomas Heyward, Jr.,*] and those from Georgia [*Lyman Hall, George Walton, and Button Gwinnett*] would have been among those who made the pernicious argument to Thomas Jefferson, John Adams, and the remaining delegates in the Continental Congress that the words attributing freedom to the Negro slaves be stricken from the document in its entirety (See, Signers of the Declaration).

Here the theory of acceptable losses is reconstituted to be set before all men and women the idea that some but not all can and will have the access to prosperity, which shall be based on the capitalistic enterprise and individual rights for some but not for all, and to afford the difference for some shall be based on racial factors alone is the ruse within the democratic society being forged. Yet the ruse would be to allow this reconstruction of imperialistic thought to exercise its meaning by asserting to the former servant that if he or she lacks the resolve to achieve the financial proprietary status, he or she would be afforded the position of the latter, even if his or her state of improvised conditions went unchanged, still would be better than that of the Negro slave. To be poor and white is greater than that to be a Negro slave because they have been assigned to the permanent under caste in the American democratic society forthwith.

From here will be the beginning of a series of compromises that would continue the tyrannical imposition for the Negro slave and the forgoing theory of acceptable losses henceforth. While the Declaration of Independence had been written in 1776, it was not until 1787 that the Constitution of the United States would be formed. And again the Negro was left out. The Negro was still in chains and completely dehumanized. It was unlawful for the Negro to learn to read and/or write. In some states, particularly in the South, if a Negro learned to read or write, he or she would be beaten profusely, and death was not questioned.

> Appropriately it was Thomas Jefferson who first articulated the inseparable relationships between popular education and a free society. If a nation expected to be ignorant and free, he argued it expected the impossible. To the legislature of Virginia in 1787, Jefferson proposed a popular educational system that would offer three

years of public schooling to every white child of the commonwealth and then send the brightest male youngster on to grammar school and college at the public expense. But what of the enslaved children who constituted forty percent of the total number of Virginia's children and who along with enslaved adults formed the basis of wealth for Jefferson, as well as for the state of Virginia.

Between 1800 and 1835, most of the southern states enacted legislation, making it a crime to teach enslaved children to read and write. As cited in Anderson, *The Education of Blacks in the South* 1860-1935, (1988), pp. 1-2.

The imperial hand had now effectively broken off from the English King, now lay firmly upon American soil with no restraint. If one finds this argument intensely wrong and suggests England and France held no slaves, read the words of Charles Pinckney:

> The institution was justified by the examples of all the world, he said, as witness Greece, Rome, and the sanctions given by the modern states of France, Holland, and England. "In all ages," said Pinckney, "one half of mankind has been slaves. If the Southern states were let alone" (again the argument), they would "probably of themselves stop importation" (p. 203, Bowen, 1966).

Thus came the Compromise of 1787:

> The Northern states agreed that Congress should not pass any navigation law by a mere majority but must have a two-thirds vote of each house, agreed also that import tax on slaves would not exceed tend dollars a head, that slaves would be counted for the purpose of

representation and taxes, in the proportion of five slaves to three free white inhabitants –the "federal ratio." In return the Southern states conceded that the importation of slaves would cease in the year 1808.

Hamilton said later that without the federal ration, "no union could possibly have been formed." It was true and true also that the Constitution could not have gone through without slavery compromise. The question before the Convention was not, shall slavery be abolished? It was rather, who shall have the power to control it, the states or the national government? As the Constitution now stood, Congress could control traffic in slaves exactly as it controlled all other trade and commerce (Bowen, 1966, p. 201,).

The American Negro slave was again excluded from the privilege of freedom. And as history has it, some subtle arguments were made to eradicate this enigma. The imperialistic nomenclature held its own. Driven by the arguments of Edward Rutledge from South Carolina and delegates from Georgia, the decree for slavery was upheld. Research today has not revealed the idea that it would have been plausible for the Negro to emerge as one of our great leaders during the birth of this new nation, however, Christopher Attucks is revered as the first colonial casualty [Negro] who took the first bullet for what would soon follow as the United States of America Revolutionary war. While historical documents herald Thomas Jefferson, John Adams, and others as presenting the moral, contentious, and passionate voices for democracy and freedom for all, the following assessment proves to be most thought-provoking.

In *The Warrior Method, A Parents Guide to Rearing Healthy Black Boys* (2001) by Raymond A. Winbush, one can find notes from Thomas Jefferson's, State of Virginia 1787 address:

...in this country, the slaves multiply as fast as the free inhabitants. Their situation and manners place the commerce between the two sexes almost without restraint...567,614 inhabitants of every age, sex, and condition. But 296,852, the number of free inhabitants, are to 270,762, the number of slaves, nearly as 11 to 10. Under the mild treatment, our slave's experience and their wholesome, though coarse, food, this blot in our country increases as fast, or faster than the whites— Thomas Jefferson, Notes on the State of Virginia, 1787 (Winbush, 2001, p. 36).

Now by analyzing Jefferson's presentation, this argument could be clarified. If history is correct, then whites or free inhabitants were dying from disease while the Negro slave was growing in numbers. Remember the Negro slave was brought to America to expand the Crown's holdings. Only through the Negro slave's procreation did the Crown's holdings increase. Even the European servant, by impregnating the Negro slave, contributed to the procreation of the Crown's holdings. The European servant, white, free inhabitants, had no direct holding to the land or anything occupied in the land. They (whites, free inhabitants), too, were situated only along the parallel axes of race, and they were being taxed without representation. This was the romantic depiction of the historical postulate echoed throughout American history. Yet the argument for freedom and democracy sat at the infrastructure of a nation being born. And Jefferson cites the inconceivable notion of the Negro slave.

If Jefferson address to the State of Virginia was true, if the Negro slave was freed, and the multiplication of the Negro slave emerged as a free black inhabitant; then the tyrannical or symbolic imposition of white supremacy in a nation and kingdom would be dismantled.

Surely someone other than this author would have come to this conclusion. For the servant (white free inhabitants) to fight against the tyranny of the Crown only to become subject to a former slave may have been Rutledge and other southerner's belief, and the subsequent beliefs of those who made the reflexive argument to free or not to free the Negro slave in 1776 and 1787. Furthermore one may infer the white male assured discontent over the Negro ever consummating with the white, free inhabitant female. The aforementioned was employed as a vainglorious attempt to increase the property rights and expansion of the Crown. The latter would have eradicated white supremacy and placed the free inhabitant whites in a minority position under the Declaration of Independence and the Constitution of the United States if such full citizenship was deployed.

Through integrated procreation, the elimination of white supremacy on this soil could have been a plausible outcome. One could reasonably infer this was why the white female and the black male were never to consummate a relationship that would produce any offspring of this kind. Was this democracy held in abeyance? Was this considered a threat against the formation of a permanent under caste to be determined by race alone, or would this undermine the ruse set forth under the Declaration of Independence and that of United States Constitution, which overtly implied – "for to be poor and white is greater than that to be a Negro slave because they have been assigned to the permanent under caste in the American democratic society forthwith?"

This analysis becomes the enigma that remains today in the minds and souls of many white Americans. Given the evidence of this assessment, one may refer to Thomas Jefferson's thoughts on marriage between blacks and whites during this time: " the amalgamation of whites with blacks" he wrote "produces a degradation to which no lover of his country, no lover of excellence in the human character, can innocently consent" (see *Thomas Jefferson: An Intimate History*, by Fawn McKay Brodie, 1974, p.432).

Even though this analysis of our country's history is provocative, in 1787, America agreed ... the Constitution would permit the importation of slaves until the year 1808, after which time it would be forbidden (Bowen, 1966, p. 204). While America forged ahead, building a new nation off the sweat and brow of African descendants who were torn from their lands and shackled into slavery, the question of citizenship for a Negro after the forbidden period of importation would arise.

History reveals this disturbing revelation at the behest of the Dred Scott decision of 1857. Dred Scott was a slave and the property of an army surgeon who lived in the slave State of Missouri (Jordan, Greenblatt, and Bowes, 1988, p. 197). Scott, a Negro slave, had experienced freedom for a short while in the northern territories of Illinois, Minnesota, and Wisconsin while he accompanied the army surgeon during the surgeon's military transfers. The army surgeon ultimately returned to Missouri and passed away. Upon the surgeon's demise, Scott filed a lawsuit for his freedom. Scott position was straight forward because he had experienced freedom in America; Scott thought he was a United States citizen. Scott even believed he could sue for his freedom in the American court system. The courts heard his argument, and in the final analysis, the United States Supreme Court ruled against him (see Jordan, Greenblatt and Bowes, 1988, & Klein and Pascoe, 2005). In 1857, Chief Justice Roger B. Taney raised this question concerning the status of the Negro slave and/or free black men. Taney asked:

> Can a negro, whose ancestors were imported into this country and sold as slaves, become a member of the po-

litical community formed and brought into existence by the Constitution of the United States, and such become entitled to all the rights and privileges and immunities guaranteed by that instrument to the citizen? One of which rights is the privilege of suing in a court of the United States in the cases specified in the constitution… The words, —people of the United States and —citizens, are synonymous terms and mean the same thing (Dred Scott V. John F.A. Sandford, 1857).

According to the United States Supreme Court ruling (Scott V. John F.A. Sandford, 1857), slaves were not citizens and they were not included and not intended to be included under the word —citizens in the Constitution of the United States.

"Although slavery was the issue in this case, the court declared no black, free or slave, could claim United States citizenship. The Constitution was made by and for white people only (Jordan, Greenblatt, and Bowes, 1988, p. 197)." Life, liberty, and the pursuit of happiness were experiences never intended for the Negro slave. Regardless of Scott's feelings and those that others may have held, he was reminded of the stated argument. The Negro was a slave and a slave was a chattel person. The theory of acceptable losses was etched in history and now bound by law gave prevailing precedence for its continuation throughout the nation. The very notion that the highest court in the land could be so virtuous to assume the Negro slave could not become a member of the political community and he (Negro slave) was brought into existence by the constitution is absurd. It is clear the courts' view of the Negro slave and that of all blacks was not to recognize them as human beings, and those immunities guaranteed by the constitution would have granted the Negro slave and blacks such a status as a human being was not to be done.

Thus the Negro would remain in captivity while the European dogma continued. Not until the end of the Civil War would the emergence of the black man's legacy be revealed. It would be in 1865 that the Negro slave would be emancipated to the status of the black man. After the Civil War, the thirteenth amendment abolished slavery, the fourteenth amendment provided full citizenship for the former Negro slaves, and the fifteenth amendment gave the black man the right to vote. From these amendments, the black man emerged and set forth his own aristocracy. The beginning of this aristocracy first emerged in 1866 through the 62nd and 65th Colored Infantries formation of the Lincoln Institute, which is now known as the Lincoln University of Missouri and all those that followed in the historical black Colleges and Universities (HBCU) systems, such as Fisk, Howard, Tuskegee, Clark, Atlanta, Wiley, Hampton, Spelman, Morehouse, and many others were formed. Finally through these institutions, the Negro slave relinquished his shackles and confronted himself and his adversary as a free black man.

Given these series of accomplishments, one now revisits the argument that Thomas Jefferson made in 1787 in his address to the State of Virginia. If the Negro slave was multiplying faster than the free inhabitants (whites), and if Jefferson was right, then the black man would outnumber the whites—in the South particularly. Historically this is true (Anderson, 1988), especially in the South, however, participation in self-governance was not a favorable disposition for the black man. To rule with and over the former servant of the Crown was met with continual hatred of the black man. He was beneath me, so how could he govern with me and/or over me, so thought the former servant of the Crown. Even Abraham Lincoln sided with this kind of thinking:

> ... the physical difference [which] will forever forbid the two races living together on terms of social and political equality. And inasmuch as they cannot so live while they do remain together, there must be the position of superior and inferior, and I, as much as any man, am in favor of having the superior position assigned to the white race (Abraham Lincoln, 1864, as cited in Winbush, 2001, p.36,).

While this state of affairs was (Civil War) captivating, America moved through the history of military rule from 1865 to 1877 (Foner, 1998). These were the years of Reconstruction. During this period, people of color, particularly the black man, was included in the governance of this nation. This level of participation in the State and Federal legislatures, where the black man would find ownership and power were met with an overt and straight forward rebellion by whites, particularly those in the south. The subject of a former Negro slave over the former (white) subject of the Crown grew as an enigma that was met with the characterizations of the black man as a buffoon. The buffoon image began the irreversible characterization of the black man in a leadership role. Often he was labeled as lazy, shifty, unorthodox, slow, dim-witted, unintelligent, uneducated, backward, and/or brainless. This deplorable epoch carried the seed for internal demoralization about the black man's image. With self-doubt, a shattered Diasporas, and the internal hatred for himself, the black man's leadership was easily dethroned.

The black man's reign was met with the vicious destructive hand of the Ku Klux Klan, which was formed in 1866 in the city of Pulaski, Tennessee (see, Foner, 1998 and Du Bois, 2003). Race was a factor, and equalization in a democratic society was not an idea that was to be afforded blacks in this nation's government. The idea that: We hold these truths to be self-evident that all men are created equal, that they are endowed by their Creator with certain unalienable rights, that among these are life, liberty, and the pursuit of happiness... (Declaration of Independence 1776) was the tormented ideological imposition of the former servant (whites) that a former Negro slave (blacks) could be transformed from the position of property (chattel personal) to the status of a man or human being was again thought to be absurd. Given this tormented and obscure ideology between the races for equalization in a free and democratic society, the black man forged ahead in a nation where he would carve out a new beginning for himself and his family. However, by the close of the reconstruction period, the black man had again become shackled by a newly emerging system of oppression. The new system became known as the institution of racism.

While the institution of slavery was abolished on December 6, 1865 through ratification of the 13th Amendment by the Congress of the United States of America, the institution of racism became the new mantle of oppression through the use of black codes for Negro and/or blacks who had now become free men and women. Southern states used black codes to suppress the Negro and/or blacks' rights to this new freedom. The formable term for black codes is known as Jim Crow Laws. "Jim Crow laws" were the practice of discriminating against black people, especially by operating systems of public segregation (*Encarta Dictionary: English*). The author defines institutional racism as the application and/or denial of privileges and access to all other privileges that are accessible and available to others who are not subjects of the identified racial group where such conditions are directly and indirectly employed and/or denied by one racial group above another."

Even under these rules of engagement, black people embraced their emancipation and continued their quest for full citizenship. In

1896, the hour and day became known as the Plessey versus Ferguson era. Separate but equal became the doctrine of the time, and the institution of racism is situated in the American Diaspora through a legal procedure. Again America chooses to label the Negro and/or black man as a separate but equal citizen who shall be again regulated to the status of an underclass (caste) being and to hold him/her up within a hierarchy of civil society only to be situated at the bottom of this new democratic platform. This is the platform for the continuation of the theory of acceptable losses as declared by the author of this text.

Upon until now, the nation wondered how it would proceed. Freedom for the Negro slave had come at a compelling price. The ruse was temporally exposed. The Civil War revealed the thwarted conditions of the white man's central development. Yet so eloquently shaped was the essence of his (white men) existence that for him (white men) to choose to believe that his (white men) superiority was vested in his race alone became the central underpinning exposing the disenfranchised white male who was illiterate, poor, and uneducated during this time [*for to be poor and white is greater than that to be a Negro slave because they have been assigned to the permanent under caste in the American democratic society forthwith*]. Therefore echoes of segregation: black man, go to the rear, use the back door; this fountain is for whites only, no sitting at the lunch counter; eat outback —reverberated throughout America and separate schools and restrooms for colored people became commonplace. Vested in this reconstruction for the theory of acceptable losses was to never reveal they (whites) were the vagrants predestined to be the under caste of the Crown's great fortune in America and not the Negro slave. Divided by this reasoning, the North and South came together to equally embrace what has become known as the lost cause.

History declared the southern states of the confederacy as a group of states who committed treason against the union, yet the resolve for this epoch in American history galvanized the southern states to declare an honorable victory for a lost cause. This predicament gave rise to southern states to emboldened their slain comrades and survivors and document them in history as valiant, noble, and esteemed leaders for a nation wrought with condescension toward the Negro slave. From this exercise, they would re-embrace the aforementioned ruse and unite again with a clairvoyance call *[for to be poor and white is greater than that to be a Negro slave because they have been assigned to the permanent under caste in the American democratic society forthwith]*, and from there, the theory of acceptable losses would be placed at the doorsteps of the Negro into perpetuity.

This period of legal degradation and segregation lasted for fifty-eight years. From 1896 until 1954, the black man and his offspring would be discouraged from thinking about and/or reaching above any reasonable level of respectability outside his or her own community (Anderson, 1988). Faced with this painful level of humiliation for civil liberties, the black man would be restricted to his community and a new set of leaders would emerge that would transcend a new democracy in America. The most notable would be Rosa Parks, Martin Luther King Jr., and Malcolm X. Due to the injustices placed upon black citizens of color, particularly the black man's women, the strength of a nation would be examined. The question of the day in 1954 would be will the black man once again stand quietly by while these exclusionary laws continued to eradicate the human decency of his race, or would he engage in the argument for insurrection? One held for peaceful change through civil disobedience and nonviolence (Martin Luther King Jr.) while the other held for change by any means necessary (Malcolm X), (see Branch, 2006).

Not until 1954 under the Brown versus Board of Education, Topeka, Kansas, and the Montgomery Boycott of 1955 decisions would segregation be aggressively challenged and the institution of racism be eventually overturned. Even with these successes, it was not until Congress passed the Civil Rights Act of 1964 and the Voting Rights Act of 1965 that segregation and racial discrimination would be systematically dismantled nationwide. By tearing down the institution of racism, the black man would have access to his rights unencumbered (without interference).

However, before the Civil Rights Act of 1964 and the Voting Rights Act of 1965 were passed into law, the black man's right to participate in its governance was met with direct resistance through riots and overt racism. Lynching black people was a common event, and even President F. D. Roosevelt refused to address the problem. During this period of history when Jim Crow ruled and whites held the position of superiority based on race alone, a black man named John Arthur Johnson (Jack Johnson) emerged.

History, on this matter of racial superiority, asserts that Jack Johnson was the first Negro black man to become heavyweight boxing champion of the world. In 1908, Jack Johnson became the catalyst for change as the physical superiority among the races was played out on the stage of boxing. The physical element for white superiority had now been defeated. The quest for Johnson's demise went unrelenting. In 1910, Jack Johnson defended the title he had won in 1908 against "The Great White Hope, Jim Jefferies" by knocking him out in the fifteenth round ("Jack Johnson." Microsoft® Student 2006 [DVD], Redmond, WA: Microsoft Corporation, 2005). Johnson victory quelled the question of white superiority on the physical front of overt racism, but the fear of other blacks aspiring to new heights of equal or greater resolve outside the boxing arena fueled a hatred for blacks that had been indoctrinated within whites for centuries.

Therefore the need to raise this banner of equal opportunity and equal access for a more inclusive platform in this great society would come the need to educate the former Negro slave children. The author's most notable point to this reference would come from the 62nd and 65th Colored Infantry, whose ideals were to donate funding for the construction and development of an institution of higher learning for blacks in the State of Missouri. This institution for higher learning became known as the Lincoln University of Missouri. Founded in 1866, Lincoln University's mission was designed to meet the educational and social needs of the former Negro slave (Lincolnu.edu). Afterward the works of Booker T. Washington and W.E.B. Du Bois moved to the forefront in purporting individual responsibility and intellectual prowess among blacks.

One could also consider this the beginning of the black man's transformation to the African-American consciousness. Tuskegee Institute was founded in 1881 by Booker T. Washington. W.E.B. Du Bois graduated from Harvard in 1888 and moved to Georgia where he taught economics and history at Atlanta University (Barnes & Noble Classis, W.E.B. Du Bois, 2003). While Booker T. Washington's general belief was the black man's window to equalization and acceptance in this nation was predicated on individual responsibility by learning a specific trade and/or skills, such as carpentry, masonry, etc., he further argued this point as the fundamental basis for the black man to become a contributing member of this great society. Du Bois, on the other hand, articulated the need to develop not only the individual's manual capacity to contribute to this great society but also the need for the black man to contribute intellectually to the scholarly realms of public discourse. One may find Washington and Du Bois' ideals intrinsic in their scope of development and offer the work of Dr. Nathan B. Young, an educator who sought the help of W.E.B. Du Bois in 1920. Here Dr. Nathan B. Young, president of Lincoln University (1920), recruited and developed a faculty of black scholars on the campus of Lincoln University, Missouri that was awe-inspiring in intellectual prowess. These scholars' accolades brought honor to this beloved institution and it became known as the Harvard of the Midwest (Parks, 2007).

Evidenced by these achievements, the black man remained entrenched in a racist society that was unwavering in its resolve to include acceptance of the black man as an equal citizen. With segregation and the institution of racism being deeply woven into America's fabric as a nation, the theory of acceptable losses was unmistakably made plain to those of African descent. This theory of acceptable losses was further realized through America's education system for the black man's children. For example:

> In the 1877 Georgia constitution, public education was still limited to elementary school. Again most Georgians (sic whites) believed that education beyond the eighth grade was not particularly useful, especially when adolescent's time could be better spent at work. They also felt that too much schooling might cause teenagers to be dissatisfied with their lot in life, and worst of all, to long for a much better one.
>
> The constitution of 1877 also called for segregation of schools. From then until the 1950s, black students would be left to be schooled, for the most part, in second-rate school buildings, to be given outdated materials and equipment, and to be taught by teachers who were often underpaid. As cited in *Georgia: The History of an American State*; London, B.B., 1999, p. 373.

However short-sighted this thinking may have been, the lack of educational matriculation for poor white students was just as deplorable as it was for black children. The elite waged the provision of ignorance upon the masses, and the solace would be found within the ruse *[for to be poor and white is greater than that to be a Negro slave because they have been assigned to the permanent under caste in the American democratic society forthwith]*. As such the author raises the proceeding question: would any child, black or white, long for more if he, too, was educated beyond the eighth grade?

How white people treated and thought of other white people was a significant under thought. Education was for the elite white population and not a perspective to be pursued by poor whites. Ignorance is astounding, but it should not be prevailing. Such an example can best be explained through the assumptions of historical records. And that historical assumption is that all white people were literate and able to read during the early 14th and 15th Centuries. The most notable argument for this premise would be made clear through the writing of Martin Luther's 95 theses. Luther, a man of humble beginnings, was born to a moderately prosperous peasant family in 1483 in the community of Eisleben in Saxony-Anhalt, Germany (see *World History People and Nations*, Mazour and Peoples, 1990). The central position for Luther's argument thus fell upon the illiteracy of the poor white peasants who were not able and/or allowed to read the Bible for themselves. The argument preceded through the fallacy of teachings set forth by the German Dominican friar named Johann Tetzel, who by all accounts held his approval from Pope Leo X.

> Pope Leo X continued the rebuilding of St. Peter's Basilica in Rome. The pope charged an enthusiastic monk named Johann Tetzel with raising funds in Northern Germany. Using a technique that had become accepted

in the church, Tetzel asked people to buy indulgences or pardons from punishment for sin. Indulgences, part of the sacrament of penance, had originally been a reward for exceptionally pious deeds, such as helping a poor person go on a Crusade. Renaissance [sic *the rediscovery of the literature of Greece and Rome*] popes, however, sold indulgences simply to raise money (Mazour and Peoples, 1990, p 333).

The act of purchasing an indulgence for the pardoning of your sins led Martin Luther to the truth about the poor white people's depth of illiteracy. This prevailing narrative gave pause to the notion that if they could read the Bible for themselves, they would have known "…that all the ceremonies and good deeds made no difference in saving a sinner. The only thing that counted, Luther believed, "was an inner faith in God" (Mazour and Peoples, 1990, pp. 333).

> On the basis of this new insight, he developed beliefs that later became known as Lutheranism. Luther believed that a simple faith could lead everyone to salvation. Thus he believed Tetzel [sic *and Pope Leo X*] committed a criminal act by asking poor people to give up their precious money for false promises of forgiveness. In 1517, Luther challenged Tetzel [sic *and Pope Leo X*] by posting on the church door at Wittenburg 95 theses, or statements, about indulgences. …In 1522, while under the protection of Frederick the Wise, Luther translated the New Testament of the Bible into German. By 1534, he had translated the entire Bible from Hebrew and Greek. Now all the literate Christians in Germany could read the Bible for themselves.

The romantic position inserted here is "all the Christians in Germany." What about the other Christians and/or other poor whites in England and other countries, could they and/or were they capable of reading? If at all, some may have been capable of writing their name, but reading with a critical application, I think not. Historical records do not support this notion. And the American story does not support this act either. Education for the common man in America beyond the elementary years would not take hold until after the Civil War, and the lost cause places this historical context in its most visible space. The premise for this insight was most egregious embedded under the imperialist rule of the Monarchs of England. Even when one considered the founding fathers signing the Declaration of Independence, where John Hancock, who was most notable for being identified as the first to sign this decree and described as a rich (White) shipping merchant, he and all other signers were servants to the Crown and this very act in and of itself was an act of treason against the Crown. The argument was malevolent because even they could not buy their way out of servitude, and the position of lower caste was not for sale to these peasant class citizens of England regardless of their newfound wealth and/or modest educational gains of the time.

More evidence for this perspective is seen through the works of James D. Anderson, *The Education of Blacks in the South 1860-1935*, 1988. According to Anderson, J. D., (1988):

> Both contemporary observers and later scholars agree that it was in the period of 1880 to 1930 that the American high school was transformed from an elite, private institution into a public one attended by the children of the masses. At the beginning of this era, less than three percent of the national high school-age population, either those aged fourteen to seventeen or fifteen to

nineteen, was enrolled in high school, and even fewer attended regularly. The National Survey of Secondary Education reported that in 1930, some forty-seven percent of the nation's children of high school age were enrolled in public secondary schools. This enrollment, in the words of the then commissioner of education, was so unusual for the secondary level that it attracted the attention of Europe, where only eight to ten percent of the high school age population attended high school. State by state public high schools was made available to the masses, and enrollments in secondary education increased rapidly. By 1934, it had become the "people's college" (Anderson, J. D., 1988, pp. 186-187).

Although Anderson's work refers to the period set forth in the 1930s, he does cite the position of Europe's populace stance for educating its subjects at the secondary level. Furthermore Anderson shifts his work as shown below to reflect the disaggregated data for secondary matriculation before 1930 with regards to the African-American child. Here the author positions the recapitulation of the lost cause for white southerners, as well as those conveyed by the northerners who once again sought solace within the ruse *[for to be poor and white is greater than that to be a Negro slave because they have been assigned to the permanent under caste in the American democratic society forthwith]* and laid haste to encumber the rights of the former Negro slave and his offspring.

By the early 1930s, state-sponsored and state-funded building campaigns had made public secondary schools available to all classes of white children. Afro-Americans were generally excluded from the American southern transformation of public secondary education.

In 1890, only .39 percent, or 3,106 of the 804,522 black children of high school age, were enrolled in high school and more than two-thirds of them were attending private high schools. The proportion of southern black children enrolled in secondary schools increased to 2.8 percent by 1910…and the majority of these high school pupils were still enrolled in private schools. Although in 1910, black children represented twenty-nine percent of the total secondary school population, they constituted only five percent of the pupils enrolled in secondary grades of southern public schools.

By 1930, the ratio of black public high school enrollment to school population reached 10.1 percent, and it jumped to eighteen percent during the 1933-34 academic year. Even then it was ten percent or less in Alabama, Arkansas, Georgia, and Mississippi. The proportion of children enrolled in high school in 1934 was nearly four times as great for the white population; as for Afro-Americans in Alabama, between four and five times as great in Arkansas, Florida, and South Carolina. The disparity was greatest in Mississippi, where there were proportionately more than nine times as many white as black children enrolled in public high schools in 1934. Significantly Mississippi was at that time the only state in America in which black children constituted the majority of the total secondary population. By the early 1930s, therefore when rural whites, urban working-class whites and the children of European immigrants had been brought systematically into the "people's college," black children as a class were deliberately excluded. In 230 southern counties, blacks constituted 12.5 percent or more of the total population, but no high school facilities were available for black youth, and 195 other counties, with a similar proportion of blacks, had elementary schools with one or two secondary grades attached but had no four-year high schools for black children. As cited in The Education of Blacks in the South, 1860-1935, Anderson, J. D., 1988, pp. 186-188).

While the ruse *[for to be poor and white is greater than that to be a Negro slave because they have been assigned to the permanent under caste in the American democratic society forthwith]* was still embraced by the white American masses, the new model of oppression *[institutional racism]* held no haste to continue this pattern of thinking. And where the Negro, black man, and/or African-American had found this new freedom, and where they had been asserted the privilege affording them the amenities of citizenship for which Taney and the U.S. Supreme Court pronounced them as coming into existence under the Constitution of the United States, the ruse could only remain among the masses of the population, if they (whites) could achieve an upward educational advancement that was not to be afforded to the former Negro slave and his offspring.

As such Anderson's work provides the nexus for this reasoning, he further demonstrated this process by writing the following narrative.

> A major factor that shaped the discriminatory nature of black secondary education during the first three decades of the twentieth century was the United States Supreme Court's 1899 decision in the case of Cummings v. School Board of Richmond County, Georgia. This case reflected the unique oppression of Afro-American people and set their experiences apart from the prejudice and ethnic discrimination encountered by European immigrants and the more general discrimination against working-class people.

The case began in 1880, when the Richmond County School Board, after a long-standing demand by the local black community, established Ware High School in Augusta, Georgia. It was the only public high school for blacks in Georgia and one of perhaps four in the eleven former Confederate states. Ware High became a solid academic secondary school, a source of pride and an avenue of mobility for Augusta's striving black community. Yet on July 10th, 1897, the school board, pointing to the need for more black elementary schools and claiming that the schools were financially hard-pressed, voted to terminate Ware High and to use its annual budget of $845 to hire four new teachers for the black elementary schools. This decision aroused a storm of protest in the local black community and set in motion a series of lawsuits that started in the local superior court and ended up in the U.S. Supreme Court.

The lawyers for Augusta's black plaintiffs pointed out before the U.S. Supreme Court that the *Plessy v. Ferguson* case of 1896 allowed states to establish racial segregation only if the accommodations and facilities in public institutions were equal. Yet in his opinion for the U.S. Supreme Court, Justice John Marshall Harlan circumvented the question of whether *Plessy* required equal school facilities by simply not discussing the issue. Upon his belief that the school board would respond to a court injunction by closing the white high schools instead of reopening Ware, Harlan concluded that the black plaintiffs' demand for substantially equal facilities would damage white children without assisting blacks. This was a gross violation of the separate but equal principle established in *Plessy*. Harlan ruled that to sustain an equal protection claim, the plaintiffs had to show positively that it was race and race alone that led to the school board's action. On behalf of the

Supreme Court, Harlan ruled no such case was established. If this was not proof of racially discriminatory behavior, then blacks throughout the South had virtually no hope of sustaining an equal protection claim, and consequently both the "equal but separate" rule of *Plessy* was meaningless.

The U.S. Supreme Court ruling in *Cumming* transformed the promise of equal protection into a "derisive taunt." More specifically the peculiar ruling meant that southern school boards did not have to offer public secondary education for black youth.

It was not until 1945 that a full four-year public high school, which was what Ware had been, was reestablished in Richmond County, Georgia. Indeed black southerners in general, especially in rural areas, did not receive public secondary schools until after World War II. Even in urban areas, little was done between the closing of Ware in 1897 and 1930. A survey of black secondary education reveals that in 1915, most major southern cities had no public high schools for black children. Although they represented thirty-nine percent of the total secondary school-age population, black children constituted zero percent of the enrollment in public high schools.

Having effectively restrained the development of public secondary education for black children, southern states proceeded with vigor to make public high schools available to white children. At the turn of the century, the public high school, as an essential part of an organized state education system, had not been developed in the South. During 1865-1885, the need for elementary schools was so great that little attention was paid to public secondary education. As late as 1888, the United States commissioner of education reported only sixty-seven public high schools in the southern states, and in 1898, only 796. Over the next two decades, southern states, in partnership with the General Education Board, laid a solid foundation for universalizing white public secondary education. In 1905, the board initiated a reform campaign that in the long run proved extraordinarily successful.

By 1935, the majority of southern white public high schools were located in rural areas. This distribution accounts in large part for the dramatic increases in southern white secondary enrollment and helps to explain how it reached virtual parity with the national enrollment by 1935.

Black children were excluded from this emergent system of public secondary education. The number of four-year white public schools in Georgia, for instance, increased from four in 1904 to 122 in 1916. At that time, Georgia had no four-year public high schools for its black children, who constituted forty-six percent of the state's secondary school-age population. This was not merely a condition of inequality but a process of racial oppression [sic institutional racism] extending throughout the South. Similarly in 1916, Mississippi, South Carolina, Louisiana, and North Carolina had no four-year public schools for black children. Afro-American youth constituted fifty-seven percent of Mississippi's secondary school-age population, fifty-seven percent of South Carolina's, forty-four percent of Louisiana's, and thirty-three percent of North Carolina's. Florida, Maryland, and Delaware each had one public high school for black youth. In 1916, there were in all sixteen of the former slave states a total of only fifty-eight public high schools for black children. Of this number, thirty-seven had four-year courses, eighteen had three-year courses, and three had less than three-year courses. Over half (thirty-three of the fifty-eight) of these public high schools were located in the border states of West Virginia, Tennessee, Texas, and Kentucky. Practically all four-year and three-year black public high schools were located in large southern cities. Virtually no public high schools for black youth, even two years, existed in southern rural communities, where more than two-thirds of the black children of high school age resided.

This state of affairs reflected in part the relative power and consciousness of different classes of white southerners as they interacted with different segments of the Afro-American South. One group, the planters and their white working-class allies, formed a large majority of the white southern people in most states and counties, particularly in the country districts and small towns. This coalition did not believe in the education of black children and accepted only the barest rudiments of a black elementary school system, which they conceded only after realizing that the masses of black farmers, sharecroppers, and day laborers could not be forced or persuaded to tolerate less. As cited in The Education of Blacks in the South, 1860-1935, Anderson, J. D., 1988, pp. 188-198).

As the author of this text, I have highlighted Anderson's work because it underlines the relentless campaign where the original designation for the American under (caste system) class was to be placed, and it was only to be designated to the Negro class as a ruse for the poor and uneducated whites in America. Here they could find comfort in the belief of their ridiculous stature as superior so long as they, too, remained illiterate, poor, and uneducated. The theory of acceptable losses shifted from the poor uneducated whites to be laid upon the backs of the Negro slave, only became a means to an end for perpetuating the hypocrisy of democracy for some but not for all. Poor uneducated whites in both the North and the South came to understand if they remain illiterate and the former Negro slave held equal and unencumbered access to quality education, the original place of the caste system would fall upon their shoulders as it was originally designed by the English Crown.

As Anderson made clear in his work, there were only a few high schools in the south for black children to attend, and they were located in the urban centers of the time, which included: Macon, Columbus, Augusta, Savannah, and Atlanta. Even with this limited level of access, the black man plowed his way forward. After the passing of the Civil Rights Act of 1965, the imperial hand was pulled back and the unencumbered right to participate in the American democracy was availed to the African-American people. If one looks at this process, an inference can be drawn that African-Americans have been equally pursuing educational advancements only since 1954 or for sixty-six years. If one begins the count in the unencumbered year of 1965, it would be only fifty-five years.

Now America is in the twenty-first century, the new millennium, and the No Child Left Behind Act of 2001 was signed into law by President George W. Bush. A critical examination of this piece of legislation echoes eternal damnation for people of color, particularly African- American children. Let us look at some data findings.

The ruse continued, and it is unrelenting. To see this hypocrisy in action, one must examine the laws and policies for states' public-school graduation requirements. In Georgia students were required to pass five exit exams: one in social studies, mathematics, science, English/language arts, and writing. Other states had similar requirements. On the surface, these laws and policies do not seem alarming, but on the other hand, it is catastrophic. Envision this idea: if it looks like a Jim Crow law and it functions as a Jim Crow law, then it is a

Jim Crow law. If a student who completes twelve years of high school does not pass all of these tests, he or she will not receive his or her high school diploma. Now examine this scenario. After twelve years of school, a child who does not pass the high school exit exam in one of the five categories identified reverts to the position stated in the Dred Scott decision of 1857. According to the United States Supreme Court, slaves were not citizens and they were not included and not intended to be included under the word citizen in the Constitution of the United States. Life, liberty, and the pursuit of happiness were experiences never intended for the Negro slave.

Oh, yes, the African-American has citizenship, however, his/her probability for graduating from high school, access to college, technical schools, and greater employment opportunities is forever destabilized under the No Child Left Behind Act of 2001. Here again lies the acceptable loss theory, and it is legal. Continuous research reveals there are numerous accounts of data that demonstrates the African-American child is disproportionately affected by the No Child Left Behind Act of 2001. The African-American child sits at the forefront of this horrible law. With each exit exam, the effects of the No Child Left Behind Act of 2001 gradually internalizes in each child who does not pass a sense of self-rejection—self-rejection that begins with the third-grade test and continues through tests in fifth-grade, eighth-grade, and the culminating high school exit exams.

The theory of acceptable losses reaches further and spills out onto the landscape of foreign policy. For if the United States is the father of democracy, one must question America's imperfections. How can America's treatment of its citizenry be considered a beam of light that illuminates the globe? Some would say that if democracy is what America gave the Negro, the Black man, the African-American, and the Indian, then it is a democracy that most would not want. Through the destruction of their Diasporas, American democracy stripped these people of their cultures and left them in the abyss.

These ideologies are being reverberated throughout the world and can no longer be hidden, disguised, and/or ignored. Democracy must be held accountable both in America and abroad. We Americans can no longer afford to exclude, misrepresent, and/or show a lack of understanding for those who by race, ethnicity, and/or color alone is treated as acceptable losses within any democratic society.

Today we have an opportunity to start a new beginning right here in America. The Negro, the black man, and/or the African-American can no longer be considered an acceptable loss. One's character should be the principal component that will determine this new democracy. The character of a diverse democracy should be totally committed to confronting the imperfections found in its misunderstanding of others. It is not a war that will be raged but diplomacy wherein civil disobedience shall serve as the table for resurrection for thoughts of tolerance and inclusion. The Negro helped to give this nation its foothold in building a democratic society, and it is now time for the nation to reject those who would embrace the idea of a democracy that is based on hatred. Furthermore America must revisit and change those laws that are intrusive and ineffective when the education of the African-American child is being marginalized. When laws and policies disproportionately affect one group of citizens over another, particularly those in the education realm, the theory of acceptable losses consumes our nation, and one group of citizens is removed from that great ideal for life, liberty, and the pursuit of happiness is lost forever.

As we have moved forward in this new millennium, one may refer to the works of Catherine Drinker Bowen (1986), Miracle at Philadelphia, The Story of the Constitutional Convention May to September 1787. While there is this romantic depiction for a noble gesture to engage a historical recapitulation of events that would bring forward this historical decree called the Constitution of the United States. I underscore the words <u>Miracle at Philadelphia</u> and ask this question. For whom was this miracle to be applied? Surely it was not intended for the Negro. The argument for an acceptable loss is embedded throughout this historical decree. After 221 years to date (1787 to 2008), the State of Pennsylvania once again became the site for public debate of a democracy that will be inclusive for all and not regulated to race alone. During the democratic primary, the high moral character of one's leadership regardless of race, sex, and/or ethnicity became our prevailing demand. During this time in our history, we see those who have been traditionally left outcome into view and employ their constitutional rights for participation in this democracy. Could it be that America is ready to move beyond its past and now truly embrace its embedded consciousness for a democracy that is color blind? One that embraces empirical evidence that all men are created equal and we should judge them based on the content of their character and not by the color of their skin.

America may, like no other time in our historical past, have the greatest opportunity to embrace the new millennium with new leaders and new leadership that will enable us to move beyond our distant pass and correct those imperfections that are embedded in each of us today. This treatise offers these questions for thought. Will Barack Obama's historical achievement challenge our greater society, or will he be revered as an enigma that should be forgotten? Does he bring hope for a better tomorrow? Is his message for change on target, or is America looking at the color of his skin? Are we to remain enraptured in the denial of history, even when it is in print? Does he or can he serve as a true representative for inclusion at the national level, or does he represent the theoretical disposition the European forefathers feared? Well, he makes a good argument, and history is unfolding daily. He is a graduate of Harvard, the birth of this aristocratic nation's intellectual power structure. But is he a Negro, black man, or African-American? He is not the first African-American to graduate from Harvard, but the seed he carries is a united disposition to deplore a communal argument for inclusion. Enough about Obama—time will tell if he is reduced to the status of Negro, or if this nation will turn the page and move into a new era of judgment.

In conclusion look at America today from this set of lenses. Three chairs are sitting in the room. In the first chair, there is a little Muslim boy who has on his school uniform, slacks, shirt inside his trousers, even a little bow tie. He respects his mother and father as his elders. The women in his life, his mother and sister, he treats as though they were a queen and princess. This history is taught daily. Now in the second chair, they, too, have on a uniform. Who is in the second chair? In the second chair is a youngster who idolizes 50-Cent, Lil Wayne, Ja Rule, Keyshia Cole, Lil Kim, and other rappers who have made millions of dollars making music. Here, too, the youngster wears a uniform, wave cap, fitted hat, throwback jersey, baggy pants, overpriced tennis shoes, the youngster also has ice and a grill. He does not respect his elders or know his history. He refers to the women in his life as B's [bitches] and W's [whores] and may even use the H [hoe] word. Now who is in the third chair, well, if you are an African-American then it is your great-great-great-grandmother and the question that has become a dilemma is why can't you tell her story?

Finally as a struggling scholar who shares the passion to educate children of all ages, I have held the privilege to offer some guidance to some, and I have written and prepared the following speeches or writings for public engagement. At the center of each writing is an attempt to place the child or reader at a point of critical thought where he or she is engaging others to think beyond their current or existing context in reasoning and understanding life as it has been presented in the past and for the future. These works are characterized as ***Reflective Thoughts Toward an African-American Heritage***, and they are listed as follows: The African-American Woman – A Great Reflection of Gospel, When I Was Shamed, If The Trees Could Talk, From The Shoulders, I Stand On, Remembering and Honoring Our Elders, I Am a Black Woman in Training, Who Am I, The Negro's Epilogue, The Inauguration, and Black History, I Am Black History – A Child's Story, I Wonder, Just a Boy an Innocent Child, I was born a Negro, What Am I Made OF, Why Should I Care About the Past, Wearing It Tight, Working Without A Kingmaker, and What Do You Do When - The Pedagogy Is Hijacked by Syllogism.

The African American Woman A Great Reflection of Gospel

The African-American woman has often endured the responsibility of care for the children and the mission of the church. With this regard, many African-American women provided leadership, hope, care, and concern for the faith of Jesus Christ to intercede into and unto the African-American family. From this position, the African-American woman began to embrace the church and its mission by bringing their neighbors, children, and loved ones to the house of the Lord for spiritual nourishment.

Inspired by their faith in God, the African-American woman understood to achieve these ends, she would need patience, commitment, drive, determination, and a community that would become supportive of the desired outcomes that she would seek. And these characteristics would ground her throughout her missionary efforts. We are God's children, and we have a responsibility to teach our children the way of the Lord. I give you the words taken from Paul's second letter to Timothy. It is written in *2nd Timothy Chapter 1 verses 3 through 5* "…*I thank God, whom I serve, as my forefathers did, with a clear conscience, as night and day I constantly remember you in my prayers… I have been reminded of your sincere faith, which first lived in your grandmother Lois and your mother Eunice and I, am persuaded, now lives in you also.* This is what Paul the Apostle wrote Timothy, and this is where I believe the work of the African-American woman lies and remains - teach our children the way of the Lord.

While our history is quite different from others, our trust in the Lord gives us pause for hope for humanity and decency. Is our suffering so great that the African-American woman can hold humility and despair as an argument for prominence to receive His Grace and Mercy? Our shame is in our individual testimonies, it holds no barriers to grief, for it was Jesus who taught all of us how to pray on the hillside at Galilee. If the African-American woman's legacy is to have any characteristic greater than any other, then that characteristic would be forgiveness. But this characteristic alone should not be viewed as a less significant statement in contrast to other cultures, races, or groups of ethnic background. Jesus Christ is our Savior, and from whatever forms that we magnify His name, yet they may be small in our eyes – who so ever resounds His Grace shall receive the benefit to His kingdom and we all give Him the Glory.

As an African-American female, one who is striving to do her best, I have become grounded in our faith and I find these scriptures to be the cornerstone of our salvation. In Joshua 1: 5 it is written, *"...I will never leave you."* In Psalm 46, *"God is our refuge and strength..."* and in Philippians 4 Chapter verses 6 through 10, *"Do not be anxious about anything, but in everything, by prayer and petition, with thanksgiving, present your requests to God. And the peace of God, which transcends all understanding, will guard your hearts and your minds in Christ Jesus. Finally, brothers, whatever is true, whatever is noble, whatever is right, whatever is pure, whatever is lovely, whatever is admirable, if anything is excellent or praiseworthy, think about such things. Whatever you have learned or re-*

ceived or heard from me, or seen in me, put it into practice. And the God of peace will be with you." This has been a Great Reflection of Gospel by an African-American woman. It is here I request all my African mothers, take a bow.

When I Was Shamed

My story has its roots grounded in sorrow. My true story was altered years ago, and I was left only to be ashamed. Torn from my inheritance, my legacy, my birth-right, and my land, I was placed in a sea of torment and ravaging winds. The sea came to be known as my middle passage, where my ancestors lay. Separated from my home, I came across this retched sea shackled to the bows of despair, for I knew not what awaited me, I only long to be home.

Upon my arrival, I was not alone; you see my sisters and brothers were also with me, their pain was evidenced, and our grief was abundant. The beginning of my shameful despondency emerged when I felt the strap of oppression strike my weakened frame. I heard a voice from afar call to my oppressor with a bid for my ownership. I and my siblings were sold into captivity.

This land was not kind to me, my sister was assaulted and abused, my offspring were bid upon as though they were cattle to be sold at auction. My shame and helplessness covered my heart and soul. I am depressed and filled with anguish. My soul is wrestling with hatred, and my heart looms for comfort while my mind struggles for hope. Hope has yet to be born. For I saw my brother hanging from a tree, burned as a reminder that freedom was an illusion, and I should not seek its shelter.

My bride was also sold to a family in need of a servant for their children. My misery does not hasten, it places me beneath despair.

Then one winter evening, I met my Savior, He heard my cry. Unto Him glory is divine. Wait for Me, for your triumph shall be in victory. The world has yet to see such a conquest, although the whip breaches your outer flesh, it is your soul that I seek. Your humility, shame, and despair shall become your honor for redemption. A bowed head beneath despair shameful and disenchanted shall be raised before his transgressors. I am the Lord and I do hear your cry, your shame is my supplication, and I have come to my Father's house for deliverance.

Understand your legacy, however difficult it may appear comes with a victory where salvation found its way unto your house. I remember it was the year of 1862, December 31st, where before the midnight came, your ancestors bowed before me with sweltering timbers of earnest prayers, whose arguments indulged in such words as, Father I stretch my hand to thee, no other help that I know....

When I was shamed to hold my head up, when my women and my child lost favor in my capacity to lead them as their husband and father, I found my victory in Christ. I was told your suffering is needed, do not be ashamed for I am with you, this I have promised you, and to the end of the world shall I be with you. My strength, my redeemer, my rock, my shield, my shame has only become a memory.

For now I hold this banner of blood, unto Him I give the Glory and from His spirit, I embrace my emancipation. God stepped in and answered my mother's call and hope was born on January 1, 1863. The thought of an illusion filtered with deceit, freedom would find His servant, and salvation would be made free. Remembering from whence we came gives an opportunity for the piety to hold in those who do not remember when I was shamed. It was a watch night, and it wasn't that long ago.

If the Trees Could Talk

Where the ages have passed, where the sun has set for many generations, *If the Trees Could Talk,* what would they say about my ancestors? Would they tell me to place a headstone at the base of the Appalachian Mountain Trail? Would they tell me to build a monument at the doorsteps of the seaports in Virginia, Florida, South Carolina, Georgia, and even Massachusetts?

Would they tell me my great-grandfather's father hung beneath the shade of a branch that swung out just below an oppressed society, and the life of his wretched frame would be no more? If the trees could talk, would they tell me this was the path that my ancestors walked to secure their freedom from an oppressed society? I can only imagine they would tell you in this old shack lay the bows of despair and here they called it home.

If the trees could talk the firewood would say, we gave them warmth in their hour of need, and for a helpless people, they cook their coarse foods upon our fires. If the trees could talk, they would tell you that we gave them shade at the end of their days after laboring in the blistering sun. They would tell you we witness firsthand their travels across the sea of despair and we listened to the bellowing of tears from their hearts. We would tell you they carved out their drums from the trunks of our wooden frames and played the harmony of hope sending messages calling for freedom and the insurrection for humanity. We would tell you upon this land your ancestors fought a good fight never wavering in their belief that one day, life for them and their offspring would be better than the one that they were experiencing.

If the trees could talk, they would say the southern hemisphere of western society would soon come to end, where your ancestors would be bound nor more by the chains of desolation, and their despondency would be lifted from the ashes of hopelessness. We would tell you a new nation would unfold, their plight for justice would reign, and their hour of triumph would give them pause for a new beginning.

If the trees could talk, we would tell you when you pass by us, not to forget that we were there when the mothers of your great-grandmothers stood on our wooden frames and there they and their children were sold to the masters of oppression. We would tell you buried beneath the shadows of our perennial reach lay the memories of misery.

However, we would also tell you on the other side of sadness there would be a day full of triumphant victory where joyful songs would be heard throughout this nation. We would tell you the breezes from international waters would carry their conquest back to the homeland of their ancestors and the trees would say here lies your father and from these ashes, I will rise again. And before the sun would set on their stories of sorrow, the trees would say we knew a people who traveled to a faraway land shackled by despair only to emerge in a victory for humanity. If the trees could talk, what would they say?

From the Shoulders, I Stand On

We stand on the shoulders of our ancestors. Throughout our history, there are those who came before us who struggled to leave us a legacy of hope. From this depth of despair, our underpinning was formed with the sweat of their brow. Beneath the Middle Passage of sorrow lies the flesh and bones of our struggle. However, within each of us, their spirit drives our redemption. For a few moments in time and each year, we here the resounding names of those whose shoulders we stand on. Sojourner Truth, Harriet Tubman, Sally Hemings, Lucy Perry, Demark Vesey, Frederick Douglas, Booker T. Washington, and George Washington Carver.

History has not always been kind to us. We struggled for and sought out an identity. We were in search of an uncompromising end for humanity. Our refuge is found in our Savior Jesus Christ, where history revealed that it was near the Euphrates River in the land of Egypt where God grasps from this earth the elements of dirt, where He blew into its nostrils the breath of life and set forth the footprints of mankind on earth. And while our ancestors found themselves disconnected from their land, their connection with God would never falter.

Therefore we must always remember those who came before us and remind our children whose shoulders we stand on. Remind them and tell them about Madam C. J. Walker, Phyllis Wheatley, Ida. B. Wells-Barnett, Wilma Rudolph, Leontyne Price, Constance Baker, Hattie McDaniel, Edmonia Lewis, Elisabeth Duncan, Mary McLeod Bethune, Shirley Chisholm, and Dorothy I. Height.

Tell them we should never forget the story of the 62nd and 65th Colored Infantrymen who founded Lincoln University in Missouri. Tell them W. E. B. Du Bois was an intellectual. Tell them the stories of A. Phillip Randolph, and Maya Angelou. Keep their minds fresh with the history of Malcolm X, Ralph David Abernathy, and Martin Luther King Jr., don't let the dream fall into the abyss.

Our history is too valuable to be lost by not sharing it with our children, for these are the shoulders of the men and women that we stand on. Our experiences today could only be dreamed about by our ancestors. Our history reminds us of why we were told to go to school. While we began to read aloud and calling words for memorization, it would be the critical thinking that would unfold and lead us to a new meaning of consciousness. Lies cannot be told to one who understands the language and its usage. Our history tells us this nation was built on the sweat and brow of our ancestors' labor and it wasn't paid for with dollars and cents.

Tell them to remember their history, tell them to revisit the civil rights movement, take them to the King Center, the George Washington Carver Museum, and engage them with the rich history of the Tuskegee Institute. Tell them they have an honor to uphold and a responsibility to lead. And above all, make sure you tell them their struggle is not over. What remains is your labor of love for the next generation and heretofore comes your watch. Be good, be virtuous, and be resolved in your convictions toward humanity. Our legacy depends on this continuation.

Remembering and Honoring Our Elders

It is written in the scripture, Exodus 20th chapter and 12th verse: Honor thy father and mother: that thy days be long upon the land which the Lord thy God giveth thee. This is the fifth commandment of the Ten Commandments handed down by God and given to Moses on Mount Sinai. It is from this directive I make this honorable attempt to bring reflective thoughts of our elders enduring love, compassion, obedience, and sacrifice, for they have paved the way for us to follow.

As far back as I can remember, my elders have shared their faith in Jesus Christ. They provided the underpinning for our belief in Christianity. Throughout their lives, they have lived through numerous wars, world depression, and several recessions. Their enduring struggles have paved the way for many of us to enjoy the fruits of their intense labor and from their sacrifices, we have enjoyed better days. You see I must tell the story that I remember because I have so many of my peers who have forgotten these stories and some just missed the experiences. Going to the fields to chop beans, pick cotton, pull corn, pick strawberries, and bail hay was a time that my elders labored to etch out a living while earning pennies on the dollar.

Do you recall the wage of two bits (twenty-five cents), four bits (fifty cents), and six bits (seventy-five cents) all in a day's labor? I would be remised not to recall the harvest season where they canned fruits and vegetables. Where they washed the mason turner jars and put their foods in for the upcoming winter. Or would you know that before the running water came into the house, there was a well outside from which the water was bailed? And the washtub where they bathed was in the back room. I believe the tub was number two. The water was heated by the wood-burning stove that would make the bathwater warm.

Indoor plumbing was not common; it became a luxury and something to be adored. Because the pool where many of my elders were baptized was marked by two stakes laid out by the deacons in a creek somewhere in the valley of redemption. Where they would come from the morning bench of grace, all dressed in their white sheets, and load up on the field trucks to go to be baptized. Indeed it is an honor to hold these stories and reflect on the memories of my elders past.

However, there is one other not so bright moment I must take note of, and that is the racism that was endured by my elders and I thank them for their courage and sacrifice. I am beholden to you for your work, and I honor you for your pain and suffering. I am not in any hurry to see you leave this stage of life, I am only reminded of what my grandmother said on a cold winter day: He is not finished with me, there still work to be done, and I am His servant, therefore I serve Him still, He is not through with me yet. God bless my elders and may your days of glory be everlasting.

It is through the reflections of our elders' past that we are able to carve out a future for our children. It is by understanding their struggle that we are able to bring a sustainable outlook forward. It is by following Jesus as they have done that we will have everlasting life.

I Am A Black Woman in Training

Born as a child, I will one day grow into a pre-teen, then I will blossom into a full-blooded teenager. After this I will become a young lady and then I will enter woman-hood. As I travel this journey into woman-hood, I hope that I will be able to embody some of the characteristics that are revered and those that I find so delightful in so many outstanding black women of our past.

I long to remember those who came before me: Phillis Wheatley, Ida. B. Wells-Barnett, Wilma Rudolph, Leontyne Price, Constance Baker, Hattie McDaniel, Edmonia Lewis, Elisabeth Duncan, Mary McLeod Bethune, Shirley Chisholm, and Dorothy I. Height. However, there are a few role models here that I, too, have my eye on my grandmother, my mother, my aunt, and my sister just to cite a few.

You see history has revealed itself, and it was the black woman who was victimized by the slave masters. It was the black woman's child who was taken and sold repeatedly. It was the black woman's labor pains that were beaten back while injustices were hurled upon them. From these sorrows and on their backs, black women gave birth to our noble sons and daughters. They walk the walk, they sang the songs, they prayed the prayers, and they cooked the food. They nurtured the child; they shielded the innocent. They carried the burdens of hope during the days where hope was yet to be born. They cleaned the houses; they toiled the fields, and now I stand here today.

As a black woman developing and growing, please keep your arms around me as I blossom in my quest to fill this stage. I am a black woman in training. Your love and support I cherish, keep me close to you.

Who Am I

In search of an identity, stripped of my Diasporas, traveling by sea, lying wasted on the seashore of hopelessness, I am in search of who I am. They called me the Negro. Who and what I used to be, I do not know, I was made over. I come from the land of Africa, however, my memory was torn loose and my lineage and I were separated from my heritage. I am told I was brought to this place by the sea, herded like cattle aboard too many ships bound for servitude. Who am I to want to know who I am while struggling to recapture my virtue?

European pedagogy places the context of the descriptions of men in the textbooks as European-Americans, Asian-Americans, and Native-American Indians, and they refer to me as the slave. Chattels personal, meaning property, stripped of human decency. I was born into a society that needed a foot-stool, one which another gives cause to be elevated above his own right, privilege, and station in life. Without a full understanding, I would work and toil the fields of labor without as much as a thank you. I have been beaten into submission, I have been made shame, I have lost my identity, and now I must be made whole.

Who am I? While gathering myself through the sea of humility, a nation would be born and the word Democracy would emerge. Embedded in its decency, hypocrisy would surround its nobility, and I would be compromised as a necessity for its composition. Still I would lie in its shadow as a reminder of its impotence and awaken the call for humanity. I arose on another day to capture the affability of mankind, and I became the black-man who etched out an aristocracy of his own.

Needless to say, my work was not finished. I needed to re-connect my distant past, my birthright required satisfaction. Who am I? I am an African-American who was captured off the coast of Africa and sold into slavery. I am the Middle Passage where Mercantilism hewed out the riches of American society. I am the foot-stool where a nation of men stood on my shoulders to elevate themselves and gave pause for the word Democracy. I am the guardian of nobility whose graciousness was laid waste in the valley of redemption.

I am an African-American who holds these truths to be self-evident; I am the man who rises above the anguishes of despair and gives hope for the possibility of human civility for all who seek its shelter. I am the man whose virtues are once restored, where honor to those who came before me and suffered are granted the privilege of indication that where they lay within their graves, their offspring found their allusive sanctuary. I am the seed they found on the continent of Africa, which gives my birthright to its claim.

In my silhouette, I carry the beginning of all life in human form. Now I know who I am and now you can go and tell your neighbor he who once was last has now retraced his lineage and again he knows his heritage. I am the birth of life, examine my pedigree.

The Negro's Epilogue

Not too many years ago, I was brought to this hemisphere somewhere near the West Indies. I was brought across a great ocean, shackled to a ship I do not know. Bound, tied, beaten, and whipped, I arose to a land that was a great distance from my home. Human indecency would have its way, and I would be transcended beneath despair. Hope would not save me because it had not yet been born and honor would run from me as if I were rebuked and scorned.

My name is what it is because my master gave me his. The sun has set on my horizons from yesterday's, and my tomorrow's, well, they just won't come. I have been told my services are needed to build a new nation. I will not be paid, given any credit for contributions, and any idea for which I might gain prominence will be given to my master.

Today I long to tell my forefathers the great news of our triumphs and the deeds we have fulfilled since those days of long ago. While the Dread Scott story may have been tragic and where Demark Vesey did not get off a shot, it was from their valor in our past that I have honor for you today. And where Frederick Douglas, Booker T. Washington, George Washington Carver met W. E. B. Du Bois, Langston Hughes, and A. Phillip Randolph on the landscape to freedom, I stand here today as a witness to their triumphs. It was from my mother's womb that a child would be born and be named Rosa Parks. Even though she was the only one who sat down on the bus, it was the rest of those Negro's who moved this nation.

Suffering, indignation, humiliation, and being reminded that my woman, the African-American woman, my Nubian queen, my African princess was no more than a human concubine brought me to my knees. And from the earth, the seed once more sprouted and a man named Malcolm X and another named Martin Luther King Jr. came forward, both noble in their servitude for humanity. Two African princes, neither one yet to be crowned, destined for immortality among the ages of our stories some yet even to be told took the stage of valor. Malcolm reminded the nation that far too long his seed had suffered the wrath of the oppressor and he was prepared to use any means necessary to encourage the difference. Martin, on the other hand, spoke eloquently and moved a nation without lifting a vicious hand.

Now their stories pass me over, what shall I do? Shall I lay down my burdens, down by the riverside, and study war no more? Should I tell you that there is a train coming and you don't need no ticket, you just need to thank the Lord. How about wade in the water, wade in the water, children, God's going to trouble those waters. Oh, they told me that in times like these, you need a savior and that you needed to be sure that your anchor holds and grips the solid rock.

I tell this story so much, it gets better every time I tell it. You see my apogee; my highpoint came a few months ago. Somewhere when the summer turned to fall, a black man, similar to my grandfather, shaded by a bright sunset, woke up as the President of a nation where I was told that I would have no contribution, I would have no destiny, and I would not get paid.

My brothers and sisters today, I stand before you and I am telling you about our history, I am telling you about days gone by and those yet to come. I am telling you the good news. Our struggle is not over. I, along with my peers, must keep it going. And I am committed to the task. I will study hard, I will excel, and I will be astounding.

You see this is new for some of my neighbors, confident, articulate, ambitious, driven, determined, steadfast, resolved, eloquent, and sharp. This is my epilogue and you have heard from my soul.

The Inauguration and Black History

Greetings, my fellow brothers and sisters in Christ, to God be the glory. As we continue to embark on our Christian journey, I bring to you a perspective that binds the ties for faith and salvation. During the past few weeks, we have witnessed a historic event, the inauguration of an African-American President. This campaign was run on change and the most profound element of change that we can embrace is the re-telling of American history. Often when American history is told, studied, or reviewed, we find ourselves engulfed in a tragic experience where people were killed, murdered, enslaved, and dehumanized. This epoch of American history often exhibits people of color calling on the Lord with such songs as *"Wade in The Water," "Go Down Moses," "There Is A Train A 'coming," "Swing Low Sweet Chariot,"* and *"In Times Like These, We Need a Savior."*

While these descriptions and metaphors bring cause for sorrow and despair, there is a balm in Gilead that redeems the sin-sick soul for those who without Him would go unresolved. Today we understand that without these sorrows, the Lord's work could possibly go unnoticed. When one revisits the history of this nation and finds the argument being made to remove any and all attributing factors for freeing the Negro slave from the Declaration of Independence, you may conclude this was the beginning of a story heretofore to be told.

We find this story throughout the pages of our history books, where democracy would begin with the hypocritical under-girding of an enslaved people. Embraced with tyranny, reduced to the position of chattels personal (property), declared as an inferior being, and as being brought into existence by the Constitution of the United States (see Justice Roger B. Taney), we now can finally affirm we hold these truths to be self-evident that all men are created equal that they are endowed by their creator with certain inalienable rights, that among them are life, liberty, and the pursuit of happiness‖ (Declaration of Independence.)

Moreover today's history will have a new byline, one in which our Lord and Savior Jesus Christ has revealed. Through all the prayers that were sent to heaven by our ancestors, Jesus heard their call. And this story provides us an opportunity to testify not only unto each other but unto the world where our Lord said: unto them, it is not for you to know the times or the seasons, which the Father hath put in his own power. But ye shall receive power, after that the Holy Ghost will come upon you: and ye shall be witnesses unto me both in Jerusalem, and in all Judaea, and in Samaria, and unto the uttermost part of the earth (Act 1, v. 7-8). Therefore my brothers and sisters, as it is written in Matthew 28: 19-20, Go ye therefore, and teach all nations, baptizing them in the name of the Father, and the of the Son, and of the Holy Ghost: Teaching them to observe all things whatsoever I have commanded you: and, lo, I am with you always, even unto the end of the world.

This is our command, and it is more prevalent now than ever before that we embrace our directive and tell the story of Jesus Christ.

Find a child, find one who is an unbeliever, find one who lingers with despair, find one who knows not our Lord and witness to him for our story, the African-American story, rest at the center of God's almighty seat for redemption. It is not a story that does not have tragedy, despair, and or hopelessness, however, it is one filled with redemption, deliverance, liberation, emancipation, and salvation. Go with God's speed and tell the good news.

I am Black History – A Child's Story

What is Black History? Black History is the reflection of stories told about past generations of African-Americans who walk through this land and gave of themselves the sacrifices of an enduring life. Some are of great delight, however, many of them that are told embrace horrifying images of abuse, humiliation, and shame. Some were murdered, some were maimed, some were mutilated, and many were just shamed. Fortunately, I was born after the civil rights struggle. And when the stories are told from a courageous viewpoint, I am no longer ashamed of the color of my skin. I no longer walk with my head down. I no longer sit at the back of the bus because it is required. I no longer stand-by while my fellow man is mistreated and humiliated. I am black history in the making. Therefore, I study hard, I aim high, I reach farther, and I walk with confidence. I speak with authority and I bow with grace.

I shall not forget those who came before me: Sojourner Truth, Harriet Tubman, Dread Scott, Denmark Vesey, Frederick Douglas, Booker T. Washington, George Washington Carver, W. E. B. Du Bois, and Carter G. Woodson. I will not forget A. Phillip Randolph, Medgar

Evers, Fannie Lou Hamer, and Thurgood Marshall. And I cannot forget Rosa Parks, Ralph David Abernathy, Andrew Young, Malcolm X, and Martin Luther King Jr... I am Black History, and I am living my story. You see I am the third generation and before me is my mother and father; one went to Florida A&M, the other graduated from Xavier and the University of Miami. My grandparents both finish college. My grandmother graduated from the historic black college named Benedict and my grandfather graduated from that rich empowering institution North Carolina A&T.

You see I am Black History because I have a choice, and I embrace this opportunity to become great, and I thank you all for your sacrifices. Thank you for this privilege to walk behind you and may God Bless you all who towed this line for me to walk.

I Wonder

Do you see the potential in me, or are you just looking over my horizon? Another day is being born where I can become great. I need you to see my brilliance, it's somewhere in your day. Open your eyes and reveal to me what it is that you see. Look not at my exterior frame, but instead look inside my inner being. I don't have my mirror. I am standing in your shadow. It's large and covers my dreams. I need you to stand back and help me emerge into greatness. Tell me what do you see; am I tall, will I be great, will you help me stay focused, will you shield me from my opposition? Take my hand and teach me not to be discouraged, teach me not to be aloof, teach me how to excel, help me dream, tell me a story that will help me become great and include me in the story. The day is nearly gone, and now I wonder will you be there tomorrow, and if you are not there tomorrow, will there be someone else who will help me with my day, or will they be looking beyond my potential and only staring into the abyss? I wonder!

Just a Boy an Innocent Child

Good morning, once again we come before you to give pause and pay our respects to those who endured the pain, the humility, and anguish of a misguided society. To those who gave their lives and sacrificed their all, we are grateful. Our reflections of the past remind us that we have a generation to educate. The principles of freedom require those who are beneficiaries of such an awesome privilege not to become complacent.

As a child, I stand before you in search of knowledge and understanding of those experiences that I can only read about. The distance between my present opportunities and those who came before me are enormous. I can call some of their names, yet it is inconceivable for me to fully grasp the pain they experienced. I am only a child born in an era where I can speak to my phone and get a response, write on my iPad, send text messages, and read the research that I find on Google.

I can revisit the images of those working and laboring in the fields. I have seen the portraits of enslaved people. I have read about the history of slavery. I have discussed with others a time that has passed where people drank from separate water fountains. I do not understand this era, I am only a child.

The long-suffering, the pain, the sorrow, it is bewildering to me. Yet I know I must be informed of my ancestral past. I am a recipient of someone else's sacrifice, just a boy who yearns for the relevance of the meaning of being black in America. My work is before me, and I stand here seeking your assistance.

Therefore when you see me, stop me, say hello, share with me some of your stories. I am told if you were born in the 40s, 50s, and/or 60s that you were there, just as I am here now and in the present. You were the children of my ancestors who not only knew those who are profoundly famous for our struggle, but you also know of those who were only regular people.

For example Congressman John Lewis was not the only one who crossed the Edmund Pettus Bridge on Bloody Sunday. Martin Luther King Jr. was not the only one who went to jail. Medgar Evers was not the only one who was killed in Mississippi. Thurgood Marshall was not the only lawyer in the struggle. Ralph David Abernathy and Andrew Young were not the only preachers in the group. And Hosea Williams was not the only one who was unbossed and unbought.

I am only a boy, an innocent child who needs to know. Therefore take the time to tell me your stories, so that I may bring forward a better appreciation of our historical past. We should not be separated from each other. For when you tell me your stories, I then have primary knowledge that I can use in my future references. You were there, at that moment, and that helps me immensely.

You see, I represent the future, and my innocence will soon come to pass, where I will become a man who will be responsible for sharing your stories with another innocent child. Therefore when they ask me, what did they tell you, give me something that I can say. Thank you.

I was Born a Negro

A historical fact, my father was born Negro, my mother was born Negro, and I was born a Negro. The year was 1955, the place was Cook County, Illinois. The document revealing this disclosure is my birth certificate. Nineteen months before I was born, there were nine other Negro children who were captured in the moment of history, and their names: Vicki Henderson, Donald Henderson, Linda Brown, James Emanuel, Nancy Todd, Katherine Carper, Zelma Henderson, Oliver Brown, Sadie Emanuel, Lucinda Todd, and Lena Carper. You should know them by the title of Brown vs. Board of Education of Topeka.

Notwithstanding these implausible conditions, and just eighteen days before I drew my first breath, someone unbeknown to me sat down and refused to give up their seat on a bus in Montgomery, Alabama. I later learned that Negro's name was Rosa Parks.

Before I could drink from a white-only fountain, I wet my lips at my grandfather's well. During the year 1963, at the ripe old age of eight years, I entered the all-white schools of Missouri; you see I represented what became known as integration.

Oh my God, if I remember well, it was the 20th Century where four Negro children, led by God, died at the hand of an unjust society, and those four little girls' names were Adiee Mae Collins, Carole Robertson, Cynthia Wesley, and Denise McNair. You should know them, why, because this was the 16th Street Baptist Church bombing that required the attention of us all.

I was born a Negro, where we ate at separate counters, where we drank from separate water fountains, where we used separate bathrooms, and where we sat in the back of the bus. Oh, what about those negroes who walked across that bridge on Bloody Sunday. One of them made it to Congress, you knew him by the name of John Lewis. But I can't forget that other Negro, you know the one who was un-bossed and un-bought, yeah, I remember, and you should, too, his name was Hosea Williams.

Now I have come to that final tipping point where a few Negroes gathered around a large pool of reflections, and somebody said, well, I've been to the mountain top, and he has allowed me to look over the hill! There you shall find a place of hope. And beyond that hill, lies a valley of redemption, one filled will opportunity and joy for all mankind. And beyond the blistering winds, I see an unfamiliar person, he looks like me, he walks like me, and he talks like me. As he comes close, I ask him, who are you? And his response, I am the black man, and I will take it from here.

What Am I Made of?

I am made of chitterlings, pig feet, pig ears, pigtails, hog maws, and barbeque snoots. The substance of my soul is grounded in humiliation, grief, and despair. My life is sustained by faith. My character is grounded in pain and suffering. The scars on my back have faded into my inner being. What am I made of? The spirit of God is my supplication. I am made of peace, charity, tranquility, serenity, and patience. Forgiveness is my mantra, harmony is my shield, and Christ is my Savior. I am made of the elements of dirt; my silhouette represents life form here on earth. I am made of sin and washed in iniquity. Yet with all that I am made of, I rise above the shadows of despair. What am I made of? I give life its meaning through my steadfast resolve. I am made of determination, stick-to-itiveness, perseverance, drive, and conviction. What am I made of? Where His Mercy is enduring forever, I am made of God's Grace.

Why Should I Care About the Past?

It appears each year around this time, we begin to roll out all the images of the horrible circumstances that depict and describe those conditions in which our forefathers endured. We are reminded of the era of slavery and the dehumanization of others whose skin color matches my own. We are reminded of the places they lived and the dilapidated houses they called home. We are reminded through the images of a life unimaginable, where people of color are beaten, tortured, and lynched. We are reminded of a time that I just cannot relate to.

You see, I always get my eggs from a cartoon taken from my refrigerator. I never experienced that dreary walk to the chicken coop, where I am told they retrieved their eggs. My water, it comes through the faucet, I do not know anything about a well. If you ask me what a number ten tub is, I surely could not tell you what that is. The field, in whatever context this is mentioned, I can only think of sports. I do not know what it means to get up at five in the morning and go pick cotton and/or beans. Picking fruit, such as peaches! Oh, my peaches, they come in a can.

So why should I care about the past? You see, we have more than three TV channels, and the remote control, well, it is passé. We speak to our devices and they execute our commands. Xbox go to TV, Xbox, go to movies, Xbox, increase the volume, or, Alexa, turn on the lights. You see, we have it better than our forefathers could ever have imagined.

So why should I care about the past? I will tell you. The God my forefathers prayed to simply reminds me too much that is given, much is required. I am reminded of their humility, but I am also reminded of their faith. I am reminded of their despair, but I am also reminded of their resiliency. I am reminded of their conditions, but I am also reminded of their determination. I am reminded of their misery, but I am also reminded of their resolve.

But most of all I am reminded of the shoulders upon which I stand. Deeply within me, etched in my soul is the character of a people whose hope I prevail. I am the witness of the prayers gone by, that who so ever believes in my Heavenly Father, they, too, shall prevail. So why should I care? Because it matters to me, for what others think of my past, I am grateful for their endurance. It matters to me because I am the beneficiary of those who sacrificed their lives. It matters to me because the injustices once laid upon another should not, cannot, and must never find favor to emerge again. So tell me your stories, show me your pictures, provide me with the knowledge that I may pass it on. For this is why I should care about the past, so that it never happens to us again to any of us or our children.

Wearing It Tight

Wearing It Tight," is the development of a conceptual framework to address the moral decline of public appearance and often the lack thereof an acceptable dress code found among the youth attending our public schools, colleges, and universities. It is the belief that fifty percent of one's personal appearance provides those who come in contact with them their first impression of who you are and/or what you may become. This outward show of one's self is often presented in the non-affirmative posture. As presented one may reveal these attributes through their choice of dress codes.

The non-affirmative posture is often represented by the students' dress code, which includes apparel that does not fit them correctly, such as wave caps, fitted hats, throwback jerseys, baggy pants, overpriced sneakers, ice, and of course, their grill. These negative attributes towards one's appearance are often displayed among young African-American males. However, the African-American female appearance can also be viewed in the non-affirmative position as well when she wears clothing that is too provocative in nature. These garments reveal an over an excessive amount of cleavage, skirts that are worn too short that may suggest licentious thoughts by others, blouses, and/or shirts that expose the female's midsection in a way that is portentous.

Why should this dilemma be addressed? The answer can be found in the future of one's intended outcome in life. If your goal in life is to become a musical artist, such as a rapper, this may be an appropriate appearance to embrace for your stage act. However, if your aspirations are outside the realm of hip-hop music, your appearance can affect your outcome when pursuing your goal.

This change in attitude and behavior towards one's outer appearance is predicated on his or her aim in life. Each industry has an ideological look or an appropriate presentation of self that is embraced by that industry. For example doctors generally wear long white coats with a stethoscope around their neck or in their upper coat pocket, nurses wear various colored uniforms, businessmen and women wear suits, teachers and educators wear suits, shirts, and ties, even the mechanic wears a uniform that denotes his/her profession.

Therefore one's appearance in the industry selected requires an adjustment in the individual attitude towards their chosen profession. Thus the education arena becomes the initial point for student ideological deployment in their individual concept of self-actualization. Some may argue the student's home is where the initial point for self-actualization begins and that is with the parents. However, others may argue that the greater society has besieged and overwhelmed the parents' capacity to engage the child in behaviors that are appropriate in particular the outer appearance of the child when attending school and subsequently college and/or the universities.

While there may be a great debate, pros or cons, toward the starting point for individual self-actualization, one can surely see the cultural impact of the students' dress codes being under siege in the overall attitudes of students attending our public institutions. Educational institutions are the grounds where intellectual and moral developments are implored. Students should be given all the tools necessary to be successful in life. Attitudes towards self-actualization are grounded in the visual imagery perceived and unchallenged. Therefore there must be a direct campaign to teach, inform, and practice good behaviors, and this includes appropriate dress and outward appearances.

Removing the negative stereotypical baggage can induce a greater concept of self and manifest a more confident learner in the pedagogical domain. Students who are released from the peer pressure of global fashion statements are more likely to become more concerned about their academic achievements and less likely consumed by their peers' perspectives of how they are dressed. We see this model practiced often in our parochial schools and private institutions. Here the expectations are grounded in the institutional outcomes. Students who attend and leave these private institutions are given rites of passage to better universities based on the direct development of both intellectual prowess and presentation of self.

Although there are three schools for thought: one of which is the development of the child to become business owners and entrepreneurs (parochial schools and private institutions), two, managers and supervisors (magnet schools), and three, laborers and shift workers (public schools). Two of the three schools for thought embrace a greater concept of self-actualization, the latter does not. The public schools and public institutions are being overwhelmed with the idea that a change in behavioral dress undermines who the child is or may become. This is a misconception predicated on practice. The greatest measure for a student's growth is his or her stated position of who they are and what they want to become. If one presents himself as a thug, he will be perceived in such a manner. If one presents herself as a harlot, she will be perceived as the same.

The concept of *"Wearing It Tight"* is just that; wear it in a manner that suggests your expected outcome. Pull your pants up to your waist, wear a belt with your trousers, place your shirttail inside, wear a shirt with a collar, button up your blouse, conceal your virtue, and wear a skirt that brings dignity to mind. Model who and/or what you may desire to become. Do not limit your outcome to rap and culturally suggestive fashion. Dress like a lawyer, doctor, businessman, or women. Aspire to higher ideals of self, visualize your profession, and carry forward the part in your coming and going. Think of yourself as sitting in the first chair and practice good posture. It is true you can become what you envision. ***Wear It Tight!***

Working Without a Kingmaker

Driven by the notion that we once had a King-Maker and now we have no one who is passionate about our future or willing to preserve our heritage, then how can we achieve sustainability for the progress that we have made? Through a critical set of lenses, you may review our progress by examining our history. Challenged by American hypocrisy Frederick Douglas led the campaign for African-American equality. Deeply forged in the American fabric you would find the insatiable and exasperating conditions of a sadistic paradox where people of color were not afforded the rights for their human existence.

It would take a civil war to press this sedition forward and free a nation of its compelling values for the denial of civil liberties. The Kingmakers would rise among the ranks of those who were oppressed by the zeal of duplicity. William Edward Burghardt "W.E.B. Du Bois" would rise from the north, and Booker T. Washington would take on the south providing the direction for educational enlightenment and intellectual forethought. Madam C. J. Walker "Sarah Breedlove" would undergird the economic capitalization from the north, and Alonzo Franklin Herndon would build a business enterprise in the south where they both would become millionaires. Matched by no other these Kingmakers would set the stage for African-American sustainability both educationally and economically.

Ravaged by the disparaging conditions of the south's reconstruction initiatives, Black Codes were introduced as the resolving means to sustain the usurpation of African-American civil rights and civil liberties. These codes were levied against an oppressed people of color. Under the Black Codes and through the implementation of the law regarding the Plessy v. Ferguson decision (Separate but Equal), the Kingmakers drew from the well of perseverance and resiliency and forged ahead.

Booker T. Washington would build a great institution known as Tuskegee University, and W.E.B. Du Bois would become a faculty member at the renowned historic Atlanta University complex. Madam C. J. Walker would undergird Booker T. Washington's development for the Tuskegee initiative. Alonzo Franklin Herndon would move into the Bumstead Cottage on Atlanta University campus. There Alonzo Franklin Herndon, along with his wife (Adrienne McNeal-Herndon), would transform the African-American landscape by becoming the centerpiece for the epoch representation of an elite African-American family. The Herndon's wealth and business acumen set the stage for the development of the most prolific Kingmaker for the African-American community of the 20th century, Mr. Jesse Hill Jr.

Through race riots, devastating setbacks, and laws representing inequality, Alonzo F. Herndon built a business enterprise like no other. Alonzo's son, Norris Bumstead Herndon, reluctantly entered Harvard University where he earned his master's degree in Business Administration in 1921. After his father's death, Norris took the helm of the family business and Jesse Hill closed the ranks as the final Kingmaker for the 20th Century.

I Come with Scares

I come with scares is a direct expression of imperfection. Growing up as a child, trying to find my way to adulthood, I consistently faced competing formats that sought my engagement. Understanding my historical underpinning, I, too, was an acceptable loss. Meaning what was deeply embedded in the fabricate of our nation was the expectation that I would not achieve any meaningful outcome that would or could be celebrated as a success unless it represented the disposition of a flawed society who thought the failure of the African-American child was a predictable success story.

It was thought and acceptable that I would not complete high school, or at best, I would take up a trade. College was never a part of the matrix that was intended for me. However, I would need to negotiate a prism of continuous challenges that would include drugs, alcohol, violence, and crime. The highest expectation would be that I would either drop out of high school, remain illiterate, become a drug addict or alcoholic, or become imprisoned. Death at an early age was also a consideration. Before I reached my fourteenth birthday, I would be shot, stabbed, and take an overdose of an illegal drug. I would experience crimes where I would be jailed, which would stain my character for life. I would be expelled from high school and told that I would never graduate.

You see, I come with scares! Born as Negro, disconnected from my heritage, torn loose from my lineage, stained by a criminal record, subject to drug addiction where death stood at my doorstep and sat down by my bedside. I wonder who would have thought that I would rise above this despair?

However, where the scares were deeply woven into my character and penetrated by inner soul, I would rise and say not I, not this day, for I shall expand against all the odds and remove myself from the statistical margins of failure and become a target for redemption. I graduated from high school, earned a Bachelor of Science degree, two master's degrees, and my terminal degree as a Doctor of Education.

By faith and through the trust of a praying grandmother, I rose above this level of hopelessness. I fulfill an idea that she had, and that was one of her offspring would excel in their studies and not become a victim of a flawed society's hatred for a struggling African-American child. You see, I come with scares.

What Do You Do When The Pedagogy Is Hijacked by Syllogism?

The need for education reform has become the central argument for systemic change in our pedagogical communities for decades and even centuries. Questions regarding the word and meaning of education have always challenged the scholar and the pupils who are subjugated to the discourse of delivery and acquisition of the intended knowledge to be acquired through the relationship created between the teacher and the student. From the earliest periods of educational history, the need for one to become enlightened or informed has been based on one central understanding, and that is can one learn how to read, write, perform mathematical equations, and critically think? Education is the discourse that one engages in to acquire these skills. The languages are numerous, however, in each language, there are very basic symbols that each group must learn in order to communicate. While verbal communication has its domain under the audiences of sound, there are the written symbols that require mastery. These written symbols express the sounds unheard, which in turn requires interpretations or the fundamentals one refers to as reading. Heretofore reading without synthesis is only calling words, and for many years this is what has been delivered in our pedagogical communities. However, the latter part of the educational reform debate has centered on the final piece of educational discourse and that is critical thinking. Analyzing, synthesizing, and interpreting written communications in a meaningful way that informs, enlightens, and gives pause to intellectual growth is the outcome one seeks to achieve when one engages the (science or profession of teaching) pedagogy.

In Georgia you may recall the Quality Basic Education Act or the QBE, you may also refer to the Quality Core Curriculum or the QCC. In either case and throughout our nation's history, there were several educational reform initiatives designed to engage the learners in our public and private educational institutions. These curriculum designs were thought to be the best approaches to achieving the desired outcomes that would produce highly functional learners in the global marketplace. These learners then would be empowered by their acquisition of knowledge and their skills readiness levels, in reading, writing, mathematics, and critical thinking would give them enormous access to the global marketplace during the new millennium worldwide.

While achievements were made in our pedagogical domains and more members of our great society demonstrated growth in learning an educational gap emerge among our pupils. When you examine these results, you may pause and ask the questions who were they and why were they left behind? Systemically they were left behind altogether. These individuals are described in most cases as the poor, disable African-Americans, Latinos, and other minority groups. However, we often overlook the majority populous group and assume they were the beneficiary of the emergent gap in educational achievements; they are not. Historically our educational system was designed for the affluent, rich, wealthy, and/or the noblest members of our great societies not just in America but indeed worldwide. This conceptual framework further supports the evidence that the aforementioned sub-groupings (minorities among others) were not to be included in the massive growth for the acquisition of knowledge.

Historically one may review such landmark institutions for higher learning and position themselves for entry. Glasgow, Oxford, Cambridge, St. Andrews, Aberdeen, Edinburgh, Durham, Harvard, Brown, Yale, Princeton, William and Mary, all established to receive our best; [- no -] our richest, noblest, and wealthiest sons and daughters would be our latter arrangement for admission. Yet the cry would be made for the poor, disable African-Americans, Latinos, and other minority groupings. Horace Mann has been noted as the one who would argue education is our great equalizer. Not for some but for all who seek to be enlightened by learning to read, write, perform mathematical equations, and critically thinking would be the framework our nation would build its reputation for the pedagogy we practice in America today.

Such an auspicious dialogue brought into practice compulsory schooling for all children. However, the method for instruction was not universal, meaning there was no one method to be employed to reach all children's educational needs. All children are different, and they bring with them different needs at different levels. Therefore we begin with a gap in the acquisition of knowledge based on each child's experiences brought with them to the classroom. This further means that each teacher begins with the gap that he or she brings with him or her in their limited understanding of the learners' needs based on his or her limited experiences he or she has when engaging his or her students within the practice of schooling. It is imperative not to confuse the practitioners' course content knowledge and/or the lack thereof with this analysis when explaining pedagogy in practice. Possession of content knowledge does not transcend into one's ability to engage in the profession of teaching others. It is the engagement of the discourse that transforms the learner, and not to be able to begin at the level where the experience gives reason to want more is more damaging than ever beginning at all when teaching others is your profession.

A syllogism is defined by The American Heritage Dictionary, Houghton Mifflin Company, 1982 as: "A form of deductive reasoning consisting of a major premise, a minor premise, and a conclusion." In our educational communities, it is suggested that all children can learn at a higher level. The major premise is all children, the minor premise can learn, and the conclusion is at a higher level. If one accepts this argument as the thesis to be promoted, then you must embrace your own limitations in the instructional design or the human ethological approach to teaching and learning.

The educational ladder or scale for intensification in the pedagogical community has always expressed levels or dimensions for growth, beginning with the elementary, middle school, high school, post-secondary, and graduate school advancements in learning. The graduate and post-secondary schools have always held the need for the development of prerequisites skills in academic achievement as the imperative standard for its pupils as the essential underpinning for academic matriculation at the highest level of schooling. However, it appears the methodology for advancement in schooling is now gaining ground through outside or external sources, such as political pundits, systems for curriculum development, or authorities for validation of credentials for certification and accreditation agencies. Evidence of these findings is viewed through the prism of best practices that are articulated through a language that often inhibits the practitioner and narrows the best approach to reach the intended audience, the student learner.

It is further evidenced by the method employed where we have passed through the practice of whole language instruction, through phonic development, and where we now have entered the field described as standard-based instructions. What do you do when the pedagogy is hijacked by syllogism? If we aim to teach each child how to read, write, perform mathematical equations, and critically think, then why are we thinking there is only one method for instructions? If we begin with a gap, why are we disturbed to find that it remains after assessment of findings, and why do we still say no child will be left behind? Has our institution failed at reaching the masses? Do we now give instructions to the university professors from the bottom up or the outside in without collaboration? Have we forgotten the main purpose of schooling in the 20th century, or has Taylorism elapsed? What is our purpose for schooling in the 21st century? How do we define its structures, and where are the boundaries for this model to be situated? We describe systemic failure based on standardized achievement tests. Society has embraced the illusion that the problem is in the public schools and arguments for such new platforms for learning to be erected and developed giving the title private and/or charter as the solution for the systemic failure found among our institutional environment in the public domain. How can one even think of giving this illusion a second thought when the populations among those who have been marginalized by the greater societies go unchanged? It is awful to think that one could exploit those who are least to benefit from such an audacious argument and be left behind, conditionally accepted, and removed for non-compliance with nowhere to return. Now where is the decline in the gap for student achievement, and how will we speak to this inexcusable dialogue for education reform?

Such a rigid approach to educational reform gives pause to think would Leonardo da Vinci provide his students with a canvas outlining the Mona Lisa and tell them what paint color to use and call them an artist? Or would he give them a canvas and extract from them their perspectives where they would build on their visions and aspirations to become an artist? Lisa Delpit work, "Other People's Children Cultural Conflict in the Classroom" invokes a call for a greater understanding of the pedagogy we practice in our public and private domains called school.

Our professors are our scholars and we need not say to them you have not been here before or the last time you were in a classroom below the post-secondary level was heretofore some time ago. Learning is a continuous cycle and the fundamentals should be taught at the elementary levels and depth for critical analysis should always be emerging. Schools should be designed to drive the learners to new discoveries. Schools should be sacred grounds and tremendous growth should be our witness, not fear of failure but the revelation of breakthroughs that prove all children can be successful in school. We spend so much time on testing that we fail to notice that we are destroying the very fabric of schooling and the virtue it brings to learning. We do not begin at the same point, and we all do not reach the same outcome at the same time, but our basic outcomes should be consistent over time. As a reference to the ideologues of the theory of Taylorism, do we now push the cars off the assembly line without a motor and then suggest we need a new factory? Internal damnation should not be the scars left upon any child when it is our limitations in teaching the fundamentals of learning that have not been captured. Isn't their failure our failure, too?

Now here comes the syllogistic argument. The inquiry is the same, yet the language we employ takes center stage. Remember the outcome is to read, write, perform mathematical equations, and critically think. The curriculum is driven by Georgia Performance Standards and the delivery is standards-based instructions. The methodology is under development, we have moved to a new design called the standards-based classroom. The administration, administrators, teachers, parents, and students are all learning something new. What is being taught is a methodology, and what is being measured is the content repackaged for critical thinking skills development. No where comes the rub, to be taught in grade school, one would learn to read through whole language development. For example, rote learning: See Sally Run, See Sally Jump, See Sally Walk, etc. Today, however, we want to know why Sally is running, what Sally is jumping to, and where Sally is walking to. Today we measure success based on critical thinking and application of understanding. These assessment analyses are not based on one's ability to call words but one's capacity to synthesize their experiences with the language they are engaged in. For example if one is to be assessed on their knowledge of American history, one must become familiar with the language of the Europeans. Such as the British, Colonist, Anglo Saxon, Puritans, and the English, which all represented the same Diasporas. Therefore, to reach critical mass for analytical purposes in testing any pupil's knowledge about the French and Indian War on the United States history test, they would have to know the British, the Colonists and/or the English were the same citizenry representing the interest of the King of England. Yet to make this story not only meaningful to the learner, you would need to understand your content, your students, and their external experiences in relation to your own.

The ostentatious argument that is moving a body of educational practitioners forward is the change in its language usage without addressing the underlying purpose of education. The experts are the ones who present the language change for best practices in the education reform debate, and those emergent leaders who promulgate the discourse and delivery for this systemic change are revered as critical thinking change agents. Such malicious manipulation of the English language for the purpose of learning is the farthest from the truth. Moreover we find ourselves experiencing this onslaught of rhetorical dialogue from failed practitioners, political pundits, and self-indulging critics who have no invested interest in our children and their hope is that we will buy into the illusion of failed success. Were they not there before, or did I miss the discussion on the previous failure of our public-school debate?

What I have seen and learned over the years of my young educational experience as an educational practitioner is the indisputable arguments of the elites and those who follow their path. Failure is not an option, it is a given, and when it is met with authentic success, skepticism is the platform they will stand on, for what has been revealed is unprecedented in their experiences as an educator. Success, achievement, growth, and fundamental development are words that elude those who do not fully understand the purpose of education. Grounded in their beliefs and based on their track records for recording failure, to see success when it is revealed requires the call for cheating, dishonesty, and/or irregularities of findings. Inasmuch as anyone, I am alarmed by such a tragedy, and where the fight for survival is made plain, those who are true to the passage for discovering what really works in schools should advocate the difference.

The pedagogy may have been hijacked, but it is not lost to the syllogism, however, the battle has been waged, and those of us who can make a difference must push forward. It will not be without criticism, it will not be without retaliation, it will not be without long-suffering, but there is a victory in sight and absolution shall be illuminated among our children. For the African-American child and all others who stand to be victimized by the current system of education reform, a call for resiliency is at hand. We must be resolved to take on the debate and offer solutions, present projects for success, and weather the storm of disgrace. There is no comfort in failure and there is no triumph for second place. Therefore when the pedagogy is hijacked by syllogism, take hold of resiliency and create a new path for others to follow.

However, to achieve this success on the new path for the purpose of public schooling, we must revisit the generations of losses that occurred under the litmus testing policy initiative or better known as the "No Child Left Behind Act" Public Law 107-110-Jan. 8, 2002.

Bibliography

Anderson, J. D. *The Education of Blacks In The South 1860-1935*. North Carolina: The University of North Carolina Press, 1988.

Barnhart, C. L., *Chattel page 331. The World Book Encyclopedia*. Chicago IL: Field Enterprises Educational Corporation, 1965.

Bowen, C. D. *Miracle at Philadelphia: The Story of the Constitutional Convention May to September 1787*. New York, NY: Back Bay Books/Little Brown and Company, 1966.

Branch, T. *At Canaan's Edge*. New York, NY: Simon & Schuster, 2006. *Brown v. Board of Education*, 347 U.S. 483, (1954).

"Chattel." *Microsoft ® Student* 2006 [DVD]. Redmond, WA: Microsoft Corporation, 2005. *Civil Rights Act of 1964*, Public Law 88-352, (1964).

Du Bois, W. E. B. *The Souls of Black Folk*. New York, NY: Barnes and Noble 2003. *Edward Rutledge*: http://en.wikipedia.org/wiki/Edward_Rutledge

Finkelman, Paul. "*Dred Scott* Case." *Microsoft® Student* 2006 [DVD]. Redmond, WA: Microsoft Corporation, 2005.

Foner, E. *Reconstruction: America's Unfinished Revolution*: 1863-1877. New York, NY: Harper Collins, 2005.

Hoffman, M. A. II. *They Were White and They Were Slaves.* Coeur d'Alene, Idaho: The Independent History and Research Company, 1992.

Imperialism: Encarta ® World English Dictionary 1998-2005.

Lincoln University of Missouri History Page. http://www.lincolnu.edu/pages/1.asp

McBrodie, Fawn, M. (1974) *Thomas Jefferson: An Intimate History*: W. W. Norton & Company, Inc., New York, NY Retrieved from: https://books.google.com/books?id=c4VT7_0NbxUC&pg=PA432&lpg=PA432&dq=the+amalgamation+of+whites+with+blacks+produces+a+degradation+to+which+no+lover+of+his+country,+no+lover+of+excellence+in+the+human+character,+can+innocently+consent%E2%80%9D&source=bl&ots=fasvMGZHvH&sig=4wRzmauER6Uf17nRJPgQYXgmj0&hl=en&sa=X&ei=VTtOVZnaEIO2ogTZrYC4CA&ved=0CDcQ6AEwBg#v=onepage&q=the%20amalgamation%20of%20whites%20with%20blacks%20produces%20a%20degradation%20to%20which%20no%20l over%20of%20his%20country%2C%20no%20lover%20of%20excellence%20in%20the%20human%20character%2C%20can%20innocently%20consent%E2%80%9D&f=false

No Child Left Behind Act, Public Law 107-110, (2002).

Parks, A. G. *Lincoln University: The Campus History Series 1920-1970.* Charleston SC, Chicago, IL, Portsmouth NH, San Francisco, CA: Arcadia Publishing, 2007.

Dred Scott V. John F.A. Sandford, 60 U.S. 393 (1857).

Segregation: Encarta ® World English Dictionary 1998-2005.

Stamp, K. M. *Slavery In America.* Evanston, IL: McDougal, Littell a Houghton Mifflin Company, 2001.

The African Diaspora: Encarta ® World English Dictionary 1998-2005.

The Holy Bible: The Old and New Testaments. King James Version. World Publishers Iowa Falls Iowa.

Walters, Ronald. "Pan-Africanism." *Microsoft ® Student* 2006 [DVD]. Redmond, WA: Microsoft Corporation, 2005.

Winbush, R. A. The Warrior Method: A Parents' Guide to Rearing Healthy Black Boys. New York, NY: Harper Collins, 2001.

Winthrop, J. D., Greenblatt, M., & Bowes, J. S. The Americans: *The History of a People and a Nation*. Evanston, IL: McDougal, Littell, and Company, 1988.

Voting Rights Act of 1965, Public Law 89-110, (1965). (see Thomas Jefferson: An Intimate History, Fawn McKay Brodie, 1974, p.432).

Ballard Hudson High School Retrieved from http://faculty.mercer.edu/davis_da/fys102/Ballard_Hudson.html

Dr. Sherman Bonds has over thirty-nine years of leadership experience in the human service delivery system. For fifteen years, he served in the role of a public-school administrator with a concentration in alternative schooling. His latest work brings forward his authorship of *An Expression of Pedagogy A Theory of Acceptable Losses Elements of the African-American Diasporas*. Dr. Bonds holds a Doctor of Education Degree in Educational Leadership, a Master of Education Degree in Special Education, a Master of Arts Degree in Sociology/Criminal Justice, and a Bachelor of Science Degree in Psychology.

His work with *An Expression of Pedagogy A Theory of Acceptable Losses Elements of the African-American Diasporas* is an attempt to review and revisit the American tragedy of democracy and freedom for people of color. Dr. Bonds pens his work with the intense desire to provide substantive information that may serve as a vehicle for individuals with the highest of scholarly aspirations. The contents of his books, articles, and poem provide the readers the opportunities to reflect on their historical knowledge of America's democracy. His inspiration is driven by his own story and his ambition to develop his God-given talents. Dr. Bonds is a caring and compassionate champion for the underprivileged child. He carries the torch for success for those who have not had the optimum experience in the traditional enclave of the pedagogical domain. Dr. Bonds is married and has one child and two lovely grandchildren.

Book Reviews

An Expression of Pedagogy ~ A Theory of Acceptable Losses Elements of the African American Diasporas

Dr. Bonds, using his own experiences as a student and teacher, has prepared a scholarly history of the African Americans' quest to achieve equal opportunities to quality education and other Civil Rights. A good read for reflection of the progress made or lack thereof.

Claudette Scott Rogers
Missouri Teacher of the Year 1993

At the center of this text is a theory that is sound, reasonable, and applicable. Dr. Bonds work is engaging, thoughtful, and real. His book is informative reading for current and future scholars who seek an enlightened truth.

Rev. Dr. Keith L. Reynolds
Pastor and Retired Educator

This work is remarkable, thought-provoking, and insightful. His, words, (Dr. Bonds) illuminates the richness of our society's past and places a constructive insight into the incredible legacies of our an-

cestor's struggles for freedom, justice, and humanity. His works are to be read continuously.

Lue B. (Lucky) McKennie
Georgia Retired Educational Practitioner

Dr. Bonds describes a theory of acceptable losses within a historical context and presents findings to support his critical thoughts toward the African American Diaspora. His efforts to be informative, yet critical is a must-read for all who engage in African American history.

Edward Boswell
Retired Middle School Principal

An incredibly detailed well-written approach to the history of blacks in both the United States and the world. This book is an easy read and offers some of the best history lessons we have experienced. This book should be used as a reference guide when researching black history from Africa to the United States. A real enjoyable digest for the family. Hats off to Dr. Sherman Bonds for a highly informative history lesson.

Henry and Linda Helm
Retired Fortune Five Hundred Executive and Educational Practitioner

Dr. Bonds presents a useful manuscript that is professionally written. Heretofore, the African American story had been trapped within the constructs of European thought and now it is being offered through the lens of an African American scholar. This theory should not be dismissed but reviewed and studied for further implications. I would recommend its use at the elementary, secondary, post-secondary levels of education.

Charles E. Glasper, Sr., MBA
Audit Resolution Specialist/Student Financial Aid Former Vice President of Missouri Association of Student Financial Aid Personnel